Healthy Heart
COOKBOOK

IN ASSOCIATION WITH THE HEART HOSPITAL

Healthy Heart
COOKBOOK

Oded Schwartz

PHOTOGRAPHY IAN O'LEARY

FOOD STYLING JANE SUTHERING

A Dorling Kindersley Book

Dorling **DK** Kindersley

LONDON, NEW YORK, SYDNEY, DELHI, PARIS,
MUNICH and JOHANNESBURG

Project Editor Nicola Graimes
Art Editor Sue Storey
Senior Managing Editor Krystyna Mayer
Deputy Art Director Carole Ash
DTP Designer Conrad van Dyk
Production Controller Joanna Bull

Text for Nutrition & the Heart Luci Daniels

First published in Great Britain in 2000 by
Dorling Kindersley Limited
9 Henrietta Street,
Covent Garden, London WC2E 8PS

A CIP catalogue record for this book is
available from the British Library

ISBN 0 7153 0825 0

Reproduced in Italy by GRB Editrice, Verona
Printed and bound in China by L. Rex Printing Co. Ltd

Recipe Points to Remember
All spoon measures are level unless otherwise stated
(1 teaspoon = 5ml, 1 tablespoon = 15ml). Eggs are
medium. Follow either metric or imperial measurements,
never mix the two. Baking times are a guide only, because
every oven varies. For fan ovens, adjust oven temperatures
according to the manufacturer's instructions.

See our complete
catalogue at
www.dk.com

CONTENTS

NUTRITION & THE HEART

An explanation of the causes of heart disease and how to reduce the risks through a healthy diet and lifestyle

RECIPES

A mouthwatering collection of more than 100 easy, low-fat recipes, each with a nutritional analysis detailing fat and cholesterol content

FOREWORD

If you have bought this book then it is highly likely that you know someone who has had coronary heart disease, even if you have not suffered from it yourself. Heart disease tops the list of causes of death in the Western world, and the number of women suffering from angina and heart attacks is increasing alarmingly. Heart patients receive stern lectures from their doctors and cardiologists on the evils of smoking, high blood pressure, lack of exercise, and stress, and on the need to follow a healthy diet and maintain the correct weight.

A lack of proper dietary advice is due partly to ignorance on the part of many doctors about exactly what constitutes a healthy meal, and partly to misinformation in the health pages of some newspapers and magazines, in which the medicinal virtues of this week's magic mineral or wonder vegetable are extolled, often with little or no evidence to back up extravagant claims.

Although modern medicine can improve both the quality and quantity of life, adhering to a healthy diet is one of the simplest ways to help postpone the development of heart disease, along with other lifestyle measures. In this illuminating book, Oded Schwartz shows that the stereotypical, uninspiring "healthy diet" belongs to the history books. Healthy eating and enjoyment need not be mutually exclusive, and Oded has done a service to both patients and doctors by showing how.

Healthy eating should not be confined only to those with heart disease, or those susceptible to developing heart problems. We must educate our children in the ways of healthy eating. So if your offspring are pestering you for a triple-decker cheeseburger followed by a double-chocolate-chip cheesecake, resist and show them Oded's recipes.

Duncan Dymond

DR. DUNCAN DYMOND MD, FRCP, FACC, FESC
CONSULTANT CARDIOLOGIST, ST. BARTHOLOMEWS HOSPITAL, THE HEART HOSPITAL, LONDON

INTRODUCTION

Having a heart problem does not mean that you have to give up all your favourite foods. As the recipes in this book will verify, producing inspiring, fresh, low-fat and low-salt dishes can be just as easy and creative as any other style of cooking.

Often all that is required is a little more thought, preplanning, and patience to train your palate to enjoy a wide range of foods that provide different and tantalizing new flavours and textures. Instead of limiting what you can eat, the following recipes allow you to broaden your options, and encourage the use of many varied ingredients.

For some people, the recipes will offer a radical change in eating habits. Care has been taken to ensure that they are low both in salt and fat, and fresh herbs, spices, lemon juice, vinegar, and mustard have been used extensively to give flavour and texture.

Meeting the demands for and interest in contemporary, fusion-style dishes, the recipes draw inspiration from the diverse culinary traditions of the Mediterranean, the Middle East, India, and south-east Asia – areas that have produced some of the healthiest cuisines in the world.

Oded Schwartz

Nutritional Information

The recipes in this book are accompanied by detailed nutritional analyses of calories, carbohydrate, protein, fat, fibre, cholesterol, and sodium. The figures are based on data from food composition tables, with additional information about manufactured products. Ingredients that are described as "optional" are not included in the nutritional analyses. For further information, see page 128.

NUTRITION & THE HEART

THIS CHAPTER CONTAINS POSITIVE AND *helpful* ADVICE THAT ENABLES YOU TO ENJOY A NUTRITIOUS DIET AND *healthy lifestyle,* WHICH ARE IMPORTANT FACTORS IN LIMITING THE RISK OF HEART DISEASE. ACHIEVING THE *right balance* FOR GOOD HEALTH IS *made easy* WITH THE GUIDE-LINES FOR *meal planning* AND STEP-BY-STEP PHOTOGRAPHS OF *key* COOKING TECHNIQUES.

Understanding Heart Disease

DURING THE LAST 20 YEARS, THE PREVENTION OF HEART DISEASE HAS BECOME A MAJOR PRIORITY WITHIN

THE MEDICAL PROFESSION, AND IMPROVED NUTRITION AND ADVANCES IN MEDICAL TREATMENT HAVE

REDUCED THE NUMBER OF DEATHS CAUSED BY CARDIOVASCULAR PROBLEMS. DESPITE THIS, HOWEVER,

HEART DISEASE STILL REMAINS THE MOST COMMON CAUSE OF DEATH IN THE DEVELOPED WORLD.

THE RISKS ASSOCIATED WITH HEART DISEASE

The risk factors linked with heart disease can be divided into two distinct groups: non-modifiable factors, which are largely predetermined, and modifiable factors – those that can be directly influenced by lifestyle.

Non-modifiable factors
- Age: the likelihood of heart disease increases with advancing age.
- Gender: incidence of heart disease is higher in men than in women.
- Heredity: the risk of a heart attack is greater if there is a family history of heart disease.

Modifiable factors
- High blood cholesterol.
- Smoking.
- High blood pressure.
- Diabetes.
- Nutritional intake, particularly of fats.
- Obesity and a sedentary lifestyle.
- High salt intake.
- High levels of alcohol consumption.

What is heart disease?

This term describes conditions that affect the heart or the circulatory system, generally by interfering with the flow of blood or disrupting the pumping action of the cardiovascular system.

- **Coronary heart disease** occurs when the arteries bringing oxygen-rich blood to the heart become "furred up" with a fatty substance called atheroma. This "furring up" of the arteries, known as atherosclerosis, causes a narrowing of an artery wall, restricting the blood flow to the heart.

- **A stroke or cerebrovascular accident (CVA)** is caused by a blood clot, either in the blood vessels of the brain or in the blood vessels that supply the brain, or by a haemorrhage in the brain.

- **Angina** occurs when the heart does not receive enough oxygenated blood due to the partial narrowing of the coronary arteries, and is characterized by a tightness or heaviness in the centre of the chest. An angina attack is typically triggered by exercise or stress.

- **A heart attack** (also called a myocardial infarction or cardiac arrest) occurs when the coronary arteries become completely blocked, either by the "furring up" process described above, or by a blood clot (also known as a coronary thrombosis).

Who is most at risk?

There are many factors known to increase the risk of coronary heart disease, some of which we can directly influence (*see opposite*), while others are largely predetermined. For example, the incidence of coronary heart disease increases with age and is higher among men than women. Women are generally less likely to develop heart disease until after the menopause, when the levels of oestrogen in their bodies decline. Heredity also affects susceptibility to heart disease, especially if a family member has suffered a heart attack before the age of 55.

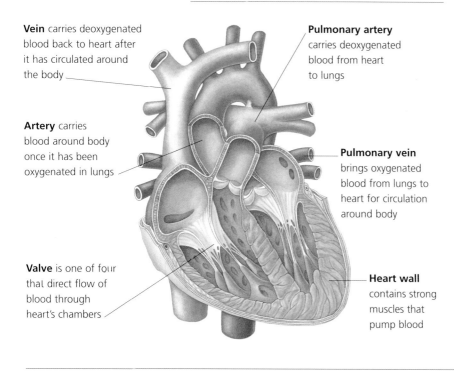

Vein carries deoxygenated blood back to heart after it has circulated around the body

Artery carries blood around body once it has been oxygenated in lungs

Valve is one of four that direct flow of blood through heart's chambers

Pulmonary artery carries deoxygenated blood from heart to lungs

Pulmonary vein brings oxygenated blood from lungs to heart for circulation around body

Heart wall contains strong muscles that pump blood

HOW THE HEART WORKS
The heart is a powerful muscle that functions as two coordinated pumps. One sends blood to the lungs to pick up oxygen, then the other pumps oxygenated blood around the body. There are four chambers in the heart, and four valves to control the flow of blood through these chambers. Problems are most commonly due to disruption of the pumping action of the heart, or "furring up" of the arteries that supply the heart with oxygenated blood.

Reducing the risks

Diet and lifestyle can influence the likelihood of developing coronary heart disease. These guidelines may help to reduce the risks.

- **High blood cholesterol** is believed to be the main risk factor for coronary heart disease and may be hereditary or influenced by diet. There are two types of cholesterol: low-density lipoprotein (LDL) and high-density lipoprotein (HDL), which actually helps in the removal of cholesterol from the body. An excess of LDL in the blood is a major factor in the "furring up" of the arteries, and can be controlled by reducing dietary intake of fat (*see page 16*). Medication can also reduce cholesterol levels.

- **Smoking** increases the risk of coronary heart disease and continuing to smoke after a heart attack doubles the risk of a further attack.

- **High blood pressure** (or hypertension) tends to run in families and is particularly common among those who are overweight. The control of high blood pressure is important in order to reduce the risk of coronary heart disease and strokes. A combination of diet and medication is often used to reduce high blood pressure.

- **Exercise** can effectively help to reduce the risk of heart disease by stimulating blood circulation and helping to control weight. Try to lead an active life: brisk walking, swimming, and cycling are examples of aerobic exercise that will help to reduce the likelihood of heart disease. Try to exercise regularly – at least 20 minutes a day, three times a week. Regular exercise after a heart attack or heart surgery reduces the risk of a further attack.

- **Diabetes** increases the likelihood of coronary heart disease considerably. Regular health checks and a nutritious, balanced diet are essential.

- **Poor diet** has been found to increase the risk of developing heart disease (*see pages 12–13*). High dietary intakes of fat, salt, and alcohol, for example, increase the risk of heart problems, as does obesity.

HEART DISEASE & THE DIET

THERE IS STRONG EVIDENCE TO SUGGEST A LINK BETWEEN THE FOODS THAT WE EAT AND THE RISK OF DEVELOPING HEART DISEASE. SOME FOODS APPEAR TO HAVE PROTECTIVE QUALITIES, WHILE OTHERS HAVE BEEN FOUND TO HAVE A DAMAGING AFFECT ON THE CARDIOVASCULAR SYSTEM. WEIGHT CONTROL IS ALSO AN IMPORTANT FACTOR IN LIMITING THE RISK OF HEART DISEASE.

TARGET DAILY INTAKES OF CALORIES & FAT

The following figures give the recommended daily intake of calories and fat for those with an increased risk of coronary heart disease. They will be useful when planning your diet and reading food labels, as well as for weight control.

Target intakes for men
○ 2500 calories a day
○ 80g fat a day, of which no more than 25g should be saturated fat. (Those with an average risk of heart disease can have up to 95g fat a day, with no more than 30g saturated fat.)

Target intakes for women
○ 2000 calories a day
○ 65g fat a day, of which no more than 20g should be saturated fat. (Those with an average risk of heart disease can have up to 70g fat a day, with no more than 20g saturated fat.)

Protective foods

Numerous studies have discovered that certain foods may have a positive effect on the heart and they should form the foundation of a healthy diet.

● **Fruits and vegetables** are excellent sources of vitamins, minerals, and other antioxidants (*see page 17*), which have been shown to reduce the risk of heart disease by supporting the body's defence system. They may also help to prevent the "furring up" of the arteries to the heart. Fruits and vegetables also provide soluble fibre and folic acid, a vitamin known to reduce levels of the amino acid homocysteine in the blood. High homocysteine levels have been found to increase the risk of developing heart disease and research is under way to establish whether eating greater amounts of foods containing folic acid may help to reduce the risk of heart disease.

● **Oily fish** such as herring, salmon, mackerel, and sardines are good sources of omega-3 fatty acids, which have been found to reduce the likelihood of blood clots and to lower levels of cholesterol in the blood.

● **Oatmeal, beans, lentils, and nuts** are good sources of soluble fibre, which can help to lower blood-cholesterol levels (*see page 17*).

Non-protective foods

It is important to reduce the amount of non-protective foods included in the diet, since these can increase the risk of heart disease.

● **Fat**, particularly saturated fat (*see page 16*), has been linked to high blood-cholesterol levels and obesity. High fat consumption and a low intake of protective foods (*see above*) increase the risk of heart disease.

● **Salt** can cause an increase in blood pressure and should be eaten only in moderation (*see page 17*).

Weight distribution

Studies have demonstrated that the distribution of body fat in people who are overweight seems to influence the risk of heart disease.

● "Apple-shaped" people carry any excess fat around their waists, which increases the pressure on the heart. It is this pattern of weight distribution that is most commonly associated with heart disease, increased blood-cholesterol levels, and diabetes.

● "Pear-shaped" people have excess fat around the hips, bottom, and thighs, and have a lower risk of developing heart disease than those with an apple shape.

Weight control

Being overweight causes an increase in both blood-cholesterol levels and blood pressure. Weight control is an important factor in looking after the health of the heart – losing even a modest amount of excess weight can help by reducing cholesterol and blood-pressure levels. Use the chart below to assess your weight. If it indicates that you need to lose weight, it is important to set realistic goals and aim to lose weight gradually. Weight-reducing diets are more effective when combined with regular activity.

WEIGHT-LOSS GUIDELINES

Those wishing to lose weight should reduce both calorie and fat intakes. Follow the lesser figure given in the guidelines if you are not very active, and the greater figure if you are able to increase your level of activity.

Weight-loss diet for men
❍ 1500–1800 calories a day
❍ 50–60g fat, of which no more than 15–20g should be saturated fat.

Weight-loss diet for women
❍ 1200–1500 calories a day
❍ 40–50g fat, of which no more than 12–15g should be saturated fat.

BODY MASS INDEX CHART

To assess your weight, take a straight line across from your height (without shoes) and a line up from your weight (without clothes). Put a mark where the two lines meet.

KEY TO CHART

Underweight You may need to eat more, but choose nutritious foods. If you are severely underweight, you should see a doctor.

Normal weight You are eating the right amount to keep your weight at a desirable level, but make sure that your dietary intake is healthy.

Overweight It would be beneficial to your health if you lost some weight.

Obese It is important to lose weight since your health may be at risk at your current weight.

Very obese Being this overweight could be a serious risk to your health. It is advisable to see your doctor or a dietitian.

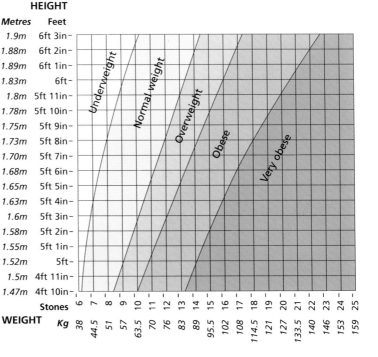

HEIGHT

Metres / Feet: 1.9m 6ft 3in, 1.88m 6ft 2in, 1.89m 6ft 1in, 1.83m 6ft, 1.8m 5ft 11in, 1.78m 5ft 10in, 1.75m 5ft 9in, 1.73m 5ft 8in, 1.70m 5ft 7in, 1.68m 5ft 6in, 1.65m 5ft 5in, 1.63m 5ft 4in, 1.6m 5ft 3in, 1.58m 5ft 2in, 1.55m 5ft 1in, 1.52m 5ft, 1.5m 4ft 11in, 1.47m 4ft 10in

Stones: 6 7 8 9 10 11 12 13 14 15 16 17 18 19 20 21 22 23 24 25

WEIGHT Kg: 38 44.5 51 57 63.5 70 76 83 89 95.5 102 108 114.5 121 127 133.5 140 146 153 159

GETTING THE BALANCE RIGHT

WORKING OUT THE DAILY DIETARY REQUIREMENTS NECESSARY FOR GOOD HEALTH IS SIMPLIFIED USING

THE FOLLOWING GUIDELINES, WHICH OUTLINE HOW MUCH WE SHOULD EAT FROM EACH FOOD GROUP

ON A DAILY BASIS. IT IS IMPORTANT TO EAT A VARIED DIET, AS NO SINGLE GROUP OF FOODS CAN SUPPLY

ALL OUR NUTRITIONAL NEEDS. CHOOSE FOODS EVERY DAY FROM THE FOUR MAIN FOOD GROUPS.

Fruits and vegetables
Eat a wide variety of fruits and vegetables in generous amounts. Green leafy vegetables and red, orange, and yellow vegetables and fruits are especially beneficial.

Starchy foods
Eat starchy foods in generous amounts. These include bread, potatoes, pasta, and cereals, and grains such as rice, oats, barley, and couscous.

Meat, fish, and protein alternatives
Consume moderate amounts from this group, which includes lean meat, fish, poultry, eggs, pulses, shellfish, nuts, and seeds.

High-fat and sugary foods
Foods high in sugar or fat are best eaten in small amounts.

Dairy produce
Enjoy dairy foods in moderate amounts. Choose low-fat varieties such as skimmed and semi-skimmed milk, and low-fat yogurt and cheese.

● **Starchy foods** At least one-third of what we eat should be made up of potatoes, bread, rice, pasta, and breakfast cereals. They should form the foundation of a balanced diet and it is important to eat at least three good-size servings a day. One serving is equivalent to a large jacket potato, a bowl of rice, or two slices of bread. Starchy foods are naturally low in fat and are usually a good source of protein as well as B vitamins, minerals, and dietary fibre. Be careful to avoid adding a lot of fat to these foods during preparation. Some cereal foods now have added folic acid, which is thought to reduce the risk of heart disease.

● **Fruits and vegetables** Eat at least five portions a day. Fresh, frozen, canned, and dried fruits and vegetables are all good sources of folic acid and potassium, which help to control blood pressure. Fruits and vegetables also provide vitamins, minerals, fibre, and valuable antioxidant compounds (*see page 12*), which all help to prevent heart disease. Each serving should weigh about 75g (3oz), so that daily intake is in excess of 400g (15oz). The following are equivalent to one serving: two tablespoons of vegetables; one apple, peach, pear, orange, or banana; two plums, apricots, or tangerines; one dessert bowl of salad or fruit salad (fresh, stewed, or canned); one tablespoon of dried fruits; and one glass of fruit juice.

● **Dairy produce** Eat three servings a day. Dairy produce is a good source of protein, vitamins, and minerals, especially calcium, which is essential for healthy bones and teeth. It is important to choose low-fat dairy products, as the total and saturated fat (*see page 16*) content of full-fat dairy produce can be very high. The following are equivalent to one serving: 200ml (7fl oz) skimmed or semi-skimmed milk; one small pot of low-fat yogurt; and 30g (1oz) half-fat or reduced fat hard cheese (maximum 175g/6oz per week).

● **Meat, fish, and protein alternatives** Eat two servings a day. Poultry, lentils, beans, nuts, and eggs provide valuable protein, and minerals such as iron and zinc. Aim to have two different types of these foods a day, but limit red meat (lean beef, pork, and lamb) to three to four servings per week and eggs to three a week. Try to include them in low-fat dishes.

● **High-fat and sugary foods** Avoid foods that are high in fat and sugar, including cakes, pastries, crisps, chocolate, ice-cream, creamy soups and sauces, and sweets, as much as possible. These foods are of little value nutritionally, and can easily contribute to weight gain. Choose starchy foods or fruits and vegetables as alternative filling and nutritious snacks.

FLUID INTAKE

Try to ensure that you drink at least eight glasses or cups of fluid a day.

○ Water should ideally be the primary choice of drink.
○ Fruit juice, fruit and herb infusions, and tea are all feasible alternatives to water.
○ Coffee intake should be limited to two to three cups a day.

ALCOHOL

Alcohol need not be entirely excluded from a healthy heart diet, unless your doctor has advised you not to drink. However, it should be drunk in moderation, since excessive consumption can cause a rise in blood pressure. Women can drink around two to three units of alcohol daily, and up to 14 units a week. Men can have three to four units a day, and up to 21 units a week.

One unit of alcohol is equivalent to
○ 250ml (½ pint) beer or lager
○ 1 small glass of wine
○ 1 spirit measure (25ml)

FACTS ABOUT FOOD

FOOD CHOICES AND EATING HABITS ARE IMPORTANT FACTORS IN HELPING PEOPLE WITH HEART DISEASE.

A HEALTHY HEART DIET SHOULD CONTAIN A MODEST AMOUNT OF FAT WITH PLENTY OF STARCHY

FOODS AND FRUITS AND VEGETABLES. IT IS ALSO IMPORTANT TO MODIFY SALT INTAKE AND TO

ENSURE REGULAR INTAKES OF FIBRE AND ANTIOXIDANT NUTRIENTS.

SOURCES OF FATS

The main sources of the four types of fat are:

Saturated fats
○ Fatty meats, lard, butter, cream, hard cheese, and full-fat milk.
○ Pastries and biscuits.

Monounsaturated fats
○ Olive, rapeseed, and peanut oils.
○ Avocados.
○ Most nuts.
○ Fish, chicken, and game.

Polyunsaturated fats
○ Omega-3 fatty acids: oily fish; liver; eggs; walnuts; rapeseed, linseed, soya, and walnut oils; green vegetables; soya beans; pumpkin seeds; and wheatgerm.
○ Omega-6 fatty acids: sunflower and sesame seeds; grapeseed oil; and corn, sunflower, safflower, and soya oils and margarines.

Hydrogenated fats
○ Hard margarines.
○ Processed foods.
○ Biscuits and cakes.

Fats The most important dietary rule for a healthy heart is to reduce the total amount of fat consumed. This means cutting down on all four of the main types of fat (*see left*), particularly saturated fats. Instead, use small amounts of unsaturated fats, which can be either monounsaturated or polyunsaturated.

● **Saturated fats** These are found mainly in meat and dairy produce as well as in some vegetable oils, and in solid cooking fats such as lard and dripping. A diet that is high in saturated fats has been linked to raised blood-cholesterol levels and heart disease. It is important to always opt for small helpings of lean meat and low-fat dairy produce, and to avoid eating a lot of fatty meats, meat pies, sausages, pâté, poultry with the skin on, crisps, chocolate, and full-fat dairy produce.

● **Monounsaturated fats** Olive oil, rapeseed oil, and sesame oil are rich sources of monounsaturated fats. Diets high in monounsaturated fats appear to cause a rise in the body of levels of "good" cholesterol, which can protect against heart disease. They should be used in moderation within the target daily fat intakes (*see page 12*). Oils and spreads rich in monounsaturated fats are recommended in preference to those rich in polyunsaturated or saturated fats.

● **Polyunsaturated fats** There are two families of polyunsaturates: omega-3 fatty acids and omega-6 fatty acids, which are both found in vegetable oils such as sunflower oil, corn oil, safflower oil, peanut oil, and soya oil, and in fish oil. They are needed for growth, cell structure, a healthy immune system, and the regulation of blood. When eaten as part of a low-fat diet they can help to lower cholesterol levels.

● **Hydrogenated fats** Also known as trans fatty acids, these are found in some cooking fats, margarines, pastries, and prepared meals. They act like saturated fats, causing an increase in blood-cholesterol levels, and should be avoided when possible. Many food manufacturers are cutting down on the use of hydrogenated fats and it is wise to check the lists of ingredients on food labels to ensure that there are no hydrogenated fats.

Cholesterol

Most of the cholesterol in our blood is actually made in the body and is required by the body for various functions. Studies have found that some sources of dietary cholesterol have little influence on blood-cholesterol levels. Nevertheless, it is wise to restrict intake of high-cholesterol foods such as egg yolks, fish roe, and offal. Reducing fat intakes and replacing saturated fats with unsaturated fats has been found to help lower cholesterol levels.

Salt

A diet high in salt has been linked to coronary heart disease, high blood pressure, and strokes. Consequently, restricting salt intake is an important part of a healthy heart diet. Around three-quarters of the salt in the average Western diet comes from processed foods; the rest comes from salt added during cooking and at the table. Cutting down on foods such as prepared meals, pies, savoury snacks, and smoked fish and meat is an essential part of reducing the amount of salt consumed (*see right*). It is also possible to retrain the palate to prefer less salt.

Fibre

There are two types of dietary fibre – insoluble and soluble. Soluble fibre is found mainly in vegetables, fruits, beans, oats, and lentils, and can help to reduce blood-cholesterol levels when part of a low-fat diet. Some foods such as bread and breakfast cereals also have added soluble fibre. Insoluble fibre has no effect on blood cholesterol but does help to prevent constipation. It is found in wholegrains and bran.

Antioxidants

These substances help to neutralize free radicals, which are thought to cause the initial damage in the arteries that may lead to heart disease. Free radicals can cause the "furring up" of the arteries that may lead to heart disease. Regular intake of dietary antioxidants may help to prevent this damage. Antioxidants include vitamins A (as beta-carotene), C, and E, and the minerals copper, selenium, zinc, and manganese. Flavonoids and other compounds also have antioxidant properties and are an important part of a healthy diet.

Sugar

Although sugar and sweet foods have no effect on blood-cholesterol levels, they can be high in fat and calories and should be avoided, particularly by those who need to control their weight.

LOW-FAT TIPS

○ Avoid fried foods, creamy soups and sauces, high-fat snacks, pastries, and cakes.

○ Grill, roast, bake, steam, or microwave food with small amounts of unsaturated fat.

○ Steam or boil vegetables and do not smother them after cooking with butter or margarine.

○ Use small amounts of low-fat spreads and salad dressings that are based on unsaturated fats.

LOW-SALT TIPS

○ Do not add extra salt at the table and use small amounts in cooking.

○ Season food with pepper, spices, fresh or dried herbs, lemon juice, vinegar, or mustard instead of salt.

○ Eat at most one high-salt food daily. High-salt foods include: prepared meals, smoked or salted meat and fish; hard cheese; canned and packet soups; stock cubes and yeast or meat extracts; soy sauce; savoury snacks such as crisps or pretzels; and pickles, including olives in brine and pickled cucumbers or gherkins.

BUYING & COOKING FOOD

THE VAST RANGE OF PROCESSED FOODS AVAILABLE TODAY CAN BE FITTED INTO A HEALTHY, BALANCED DIET, PROVIDED THAT YOU HAVE SOME KNOW-HOW ABOUT READING THE LABELS. THE INGREDIENTS LABEL IS EASY TO UNDERSTAND, SINCE INGREDIENTS ARE ALWAYS LISTED IN ORDER OF WEIGHT, SO THAT THE MAIN INGREDIENT IS FIRST ON THE LIST. NUTRITIONAL LABELS ARE MORE COMPLICATED.

What the labels say When you read the nutritional labels on processed and prepared foods, you should consider how the food might fit into your diet. Some foods may look to be high in fat, sugar, salt, or calories but, if they are eaten only in small amounts or occasionally, they can still fit into the overall balance of your diet. Foods that you eat regularly or in larger amounts will have a greater effect on the balance of your diet; when buying them, it is worth looking for brands that are low in fat, salt, and sugar. As a rough guide when shopping, choose soups and desserts with less than 5g fat per serving, and prepared meals with only 10–15g fat per serving.

NUTRITION INFORMATION ON FOOD LABELS

These are the nutrients typically included on food labels. Use the weight column for comparing similar foods, such as canned soups, and the "per serving" column to compare different types of food.

Energy (Kcals or Kj) The amount of energy measured as calories or joules that you will get from the food.

Protein (g) Because there is usually more than enough in the diet, there is no need to take too much notice of protein content (unless you are on a special, low-protein diet).

Carbohydrate (g) These are mainly starches and sugars, given either as figures for each, or just as total carbohydrate. Try to choose foods that are higher in starchy carbohydrate than in sugars.

Nutrition Information Typical Values	Amount per 100g	Amount per serving (200g)
Energy	212kj/50kcal	424kj/100kcal
Protein	1.9g	3.8g
Carbohydrate	10.1g	20.1g
(of which sugars)	(1.7g)	(3.3g)
Fat	0.2g	0.4g
(of which saturated)	(trace)	(trace)
Fibre	0.6g	1.3g
Sodium	0.4g	0.8g

Sugar (g) This figure is for all types of sugar. The nutrition panel may list carbohydrate content followed by "of which sugars" or "added sugars". This refers to all the sugars in the product, natural or added.

Fat (g) This figure is the total amount of fat in the food, and is sometimes broken down into saturated, monounsaturated, and polyunsaturated fats. Try to choose foods that are low in fat, particularly in saturated fat. Choose oils and spreads that are rich in monounsaturated fats.

Sodium (g) Most of the sodium in food comes from salt (sodium chloride). It is advisable to have no more than 2.4g sodium per day (equivalent to 6g salt).

Fibre (g) This figure is the total amount of fibre in the food, including soluble and insoluble types. Aim to eat around 18g of fibre each day.

CHOOSING HEALTHY FOODS

When shopping for ready-prepared foods or for the ingredients for your own cooking, always be on the lookout for healthy options – that is, foods or ingredients that are lower in fat than the traditional versions. You may find the following suggestions helpful.

HIGH-FAT FOODS	LOWER-FAT OPTIONS
• Full-cream milk and dairy foods.	• Skimmed or semi-skimmed milk; low-fat yogurt and fromage frais.
• Hard cheeses.	• Half-fat Cheddar, Brie, or Edam cheeses; low-fat soft cheese.
• Butter; margarine.	• Low- or reduced fat spreads that are low in saturates.
• Garlic bread and oily breads such as foccacia.	• Wholemeal bread or rolls; bagels; pitta bread; breadsticks; rice cakes.
• Cakes; pastries; doughnuts.	• Tea cakes; crumpets; English muffins.
• Chips; oily roast potatoes.	• Jacket and boiled potatoes.
• Fried rice and noodles.	• Boiled or steamed rice; boiled noodles.
• Pasta with creamy sauces.	• Pasta with low-fat, vegetable-based sauces.
• Fried vegetables.	• Oven-roasted vegetables, brushed with a little oil.
• Ice-cream.	• Virtually fat-free ice-creams; frozen yogurts; sorbets; water ices.
• Fatty and processed meats.	• Lean fresh meats (or meats trimmed of fat); ham; cold roast meats; lean back bacon.
• Creamy soups.	• Low-fat vegetable soups; stock-based soups.
• Salad dressings; mayonnaise.	• Fat-free, yogurt-based dressings; balsamic vinegar; low-fat diet dressings.
• High-fat ready meals.	• Meals without pastry or cream or cheese sauces, with no more than 10–15g fat per serving.
• Fried foods.	• Grilled, baked, microwaved, steamed, and boiled foods.
• Rich, creamy desserts.	• Fruit-based desserts; light or low-fat yogurts, mousses, rice puddings, and fromage frais (look for low-sugar types, too).
• Crisps; salted nuts; salty snacks.	• Unsalted snacks; homemade popcorn (with no fat and salt).

Low-fat Cooking Techniques

THE FOLLOWING TECHNIQUES DEMONSTRATE SIMPLE WAYS TO KEEP FAT LEVELS TO A MINIMUM WHEN COOKING WITHOUT COMPROMISING ON TASTE. THESE METHODS OF PREPARATION REDUCE OR ELIMINATE THE NEED FOR ADDITIONAL OIL OR FAT, AND ARE PREFERABLE TO FRYING AND ROASTING, WHICH CAN INCREASE FAT LEVELS SIGNIFICANTLY.

WAYS OF REDUCING FAT IN COOKING

There are many quick and simple methods of food preparation that will ensure fat levels are kept to a minimum when cooking.

❍ Visible fat found on meat and the skin on poultry should be removed to reduce significantly the fat and calorie content.

❍ Vegetables can be cooked in a little water instead of oil. The pan should be covered to enable the vegetables to cook in their own steam and moisture.

❍ Flavourings such as herbs, garlic, wine, and lemon or lime juice can add flavour and moisture to fish, meat, or poultry, reducing the need for additional oil.

❍ A heavy-based, non-stick pan will help to prevent foods sticking to the base, reducing the need for oil or fat.

❍ Meat, poultry, or fish should be placed on a rack when grilling or roasting to allow fat from the foods to drain away.

GRIDDLING

Griddling browns and seals in the juices of foods such as fish, meat, and poultry, and requires little or no extra oil or fat. It is important to preheat the griddle beforehand.

SEARING

This method of cooking is perfect for sealing in the juices of foods such as meat, fish, and poultry, and requires little or no extra oil or fat. It is important to preheat the pan first.

GRILLING

Grilling browns foods quickly on the outside while sealing the juices inside. It may be necessary to brush the foods with a little oil, or marinate them first, to prevent them from drying out.

STIR-FRYING

Stir-frying is a fast and healthy method of cooking, and a non-stick wok helps to keep fat levels to a minimum. It is important to prepare all ingredients before starting to cook.

HOT-SMOKING

Hot-smoking is a quick, totally fat-free method of cooking. Foods such as a fish, meat, and poultry are arranged on a rack placed in a wok, and cooked over a layer of tea leaves and other flavourings to give them a light, smoky flavour.

PARCEL-COOKING

Sometimes known as *en papillote*, this technique refers to foods cooked inside a parcel. This enables the flavour, juices, and nutrients to be retained and eliminates the need for additional oil or fat. It is suitable for foods such as fish, meat, poultry, and fruits and vegetables.

Cooking in parchment paper helps to seal in the moisture in foods. The parcel can be placed in a steamer or baked in an oven. In the heat, the ingredients steam and the flavours mingle.

SAUTEING

Foods that are cooked by sautéing or sweating should be moistened with a small amount of oil. A lid may also be used to allow the foods to cook in their own juices.

STEAMING

Steaming is a quick, fat-free method of cooking that is particularly suitable for vegetables, poultry, and fish. Careful timing is crucial to ensure that foods are cooked to perfection.

MARINATING

Marinades add flavour and help to tenderize foods and keep them moist during cooking without the need for any or additional oil. Poultry, meat, fish, and vegetables all marinate well.

POACHING

Poaching is a low-fat method of cooking foods such as fruits, fish, eggs, and meat. Fruit is often poached in a syrup, while meat, poultry, and fish are usually simmered in stock.

Cooking in foil works on the same principle as cooking in paper but foods may also be barbecued.

MEAL PLANNING

MEAL PLANNING IS ONE OF THE KEY FACTORS IN
MAINTAINING THE HEALTH OF THE HEART. BY
EATING A VARIED DIET BASED ON A RANGE OF
HEALTHY INGREDIENTS YOU CAN HELP TO CONTROL
YOUR WEIGHT, REDUCE CHOLESTEROL LEVELS,
AND KEEP TOTAL FAT INTAKE IN CHECK.

Healthy eating tips

The following guidelines will help you to plan a well-balanced, healthy diet, even when eating out, and they complement the meal suggestions that follow.

● Cut down on the amount of fat you eat, especially your intake of saturated fat.

● Base meals and snacks around starchy foods, including bread, potatoes, rice, pasta, and cereals.

● Aim to eat at least five helpings of fruits and vegetables daily, including fresh, frozen, dried, and canned varieties, as well as fruit juices. Choose fruits canned in natural juice and avoid canned vegetables in salt or brine.

● Eat fish regularly – at least three servings a week. One or more of these servings should be oily fish: tuna, salmon, mackerel, herrings, or sardines.

● Choose low-fat dairy produce such as skimmed milk, low-fat yogurt, and low-fat cheese.

● Eat only small amounts of lean meat and poultry.

● Reduce your salt intake.

● Choose foods that are a rich source of soluble fibre, such as oats, lentils, peas, sweetcorn, and beans.

VEGETARIAN SUPPERS

BROAD BEAN & ARTICHOKE STEW,
(*page 84*) served with rice and steamed broccoli

BAKED BANANAS WITH VANILLA (*page 107*)

MEDITERRANEAN GRIDDLED VEGETABLE
SALAD (*page 100*) served with bread,
rice, or pasta

PEACH & GINGER MERINGUE PIE
(*page 110*)

ORIENTAL MUSHROOM RISOTTO (*page 55*)
served with salad

FIGS WITH MARBLED YOGURT
& HONEY SAUCE (*page 106*)

ABOVE *Mediterranean Griddled Vegetable Salad*

BRUNCHES

FRUIT SMOOTHIE (*page 28*)

LOW-FAT BREAKFAST SAUSAGES (*page 34*)
served with grilled tomatoes, grilled mushrooms,
and wholemeal toast

SPICED FISH KEDGEREE
(*page 36*) served with grilled tomatoes

STRAWBERRY & MANGO SALAD (*page 32*)

APRICOT & DATE MUESLI (*page 30*)

CARROT & COURGETTE GRIDDLE CAKES
(*page 35*) served with grilled tomatoes

RIGHT *Fruit Smoothies*

MIDWEEK SUPPERS

BAKED COD WITH
TOMATO & PEPPER SALSA (*page 60*)
served with new potatoes and a green vegetable

CARAMELIZED RICE PUDDING (*page 115*)

ORIENTAL GINGER CHICKEN (*page 74*) served
with noodles and a green vegetable

POACHED SPICED PEARS (*page 107*)

VENISON BURGERS (*page 80*) served in a bun
with CARAMELIZED ONION & POTATO
SALAD (*page 91*)

MIXED MELON SALAD (*page 106*)

LEFT *Venison Burger*

Eating out

There is no reason to avoid eating out if you have a heart problem, but care should be taken when ordering.

When eating out avoid foods that are high in fat, including: heavily dressed salads; creamy soups, sauces (hollandaise sauce and beurre blanc), and desserts; fried, batter-coated foods; fried vegetables; pastry; oily Italian breads, garlic bread, and bread spread thickly with butter; and the cheeseboard. Instead, choose dishes that are lower in fat:

- **STARTERS** Stock-based soups such as minestrone, chicken, or vegetable; salads with the dressing on the side; fruits such as melon, pineapple, or grapefruit; corn on the cob (without butter); or seafood (without heavy dressing) such as smoked salmon, crab, mussels, or oysters.

- **MAIN COURSES** Grilled poultry or fish with vegetables and potatoes, rice, or pasta; pasta with tomato sauce and salad; Chinese or Indian meal with boiled rice (avoid fried meat dishes and oily sauces); poultry kebabs; or tandoori chicken with rice.

- **DESSERTS** Fresh fruit salad; sorbet; meringue; low-fat yogurt; or poached fruits.

Snack ideas

Many snacks are high in fat and contain very little in the way of nourishment. To avoid the temptation, choose from the following low-fat, low-salt alternatives.

- Toast with a little low-fat spread and high-fruit jam

- A few plain biscuits (about 1g fat per biscuit)

- Fruits or low-fat yogurts

- Crispbreads or rice cakes with low-fat cheese

- Unsalted popcorn or pretzels

- Ice lollies or sorbets

DINNER PARTIES

WINTER TOMATO SOUP (*page 40*)
served with wholemeal bread

CHINESE STEAMED SEA BASS (*page 68*)
served with a green vegetable and noodles

LAYERED FRUIT & YOGURT MOUSSE
(*page 105*)

———————

CHERRY SOUP (*page 38*) served with bread

VENISON STEAK WITH THREE-PEPPER
SALSA (*page 79*) served with
ROASTED GARLIC & COURGETTE SALAD
(*page 90*) and new potatoes

MIXED BERRIES WITH SWEET POLENTA
GNOCCHI (*page 112*)

ABOVE *Chinese Steamed Sea Bass*

LIGHT LUNCHES

THAI FISH & NOODLE SOUP *(page 44)*
served with a piece of fruit

MY FAVOURITE SANDWICH *(page 48)*
served with salad

PEAR YOGURT ICE *(page 104)*

QUICK TOMATO & FRESH HERB PILAFF
(page 51) followed by low-fat natural yogurt
flavoured with a spoonful of honey

FRESH HERB & COTTAGE
CHEESE PASTA *(page 58)* served with
a piece of fruit

BELOW *Thai Fish & Noodle Soup*

BUFFET PARTY FOR TEN

FRESH VEGETABLE PATTIES *(page 50)*

TANDOORI CHICKEN *(page 73)*

TEA-SMOKED SALMON *(page 71)*

ROASTED RED PEPPER & CHICK-PEA
SALAD *(page 88)*

CARAMELIZED ONION & POTATO SALAD
(page 91)

BEETROOT SALAD WITH
HONEY & YOGURT DRESSING *(page 93)*

TUNA & BEAN SALAD *(page 94)*

SMOKY AUBERGINE & TOMATO SALAD
(page 96)

PASSION FRUIT PAVLOVA *(page 108)*

ABOVE *Passion Fruit Pavlova*

RECIPES

THE RECIPES IN THIS SECTION OFFER A NEW AND

fresh approach TO HEALTHY EATING. THEY

HAVE BEEN CREATED TO ENABLE YOU TO MAKE

DELICIOUS, *inspiring,* AND *nutritious*

BREAKFASTS, SOUPS, LIGHT MEALS, MAIN COURSES, AND

DESSERTS. THERE ARE ALSO *innovative ideas*

FOR *low-fat* SALAD DRESSINGS, SAUCES, AND

STOCKS THAT WILL HELP YOU TO TRANSFORM

ORDINARY DISHES INTO *gourmet meals*.

Papaya & Banana Smoothie

THIS VIBRANT AND REFRESHING DRINK MAKES A NUTRITIOUS AND INVIGORATING START TO THE DAY. TO FURTHER BOOST ITS VITAMIN AND MINERAL CONTENT, ADD OATS OR ANOTHER SIMILAR GRAIN WHEN BLENDING THE FRUITS.

✱ STAR INGREDIENT

Papaya is a rich source of vitamin C and beta-carotene, both of which are antioxidants that may help to prevent cell damage and heart disease.

EACH SERVING PROVIDES:

○ Calories 160

○ Protein 7g

○ Carbohydrate 35g
   Fibre 4g

○ Total Fat <1g
   Saturated Fat <1g
   Polyunsaturated Fat <1g
   Monounsaturated Fat <1g

○ Cholesterol 0mg

○ Sodium 44mg

SERVING TIP

It is important to drink juices and smoothies soon after they are made since their nutritional value quickly diminishes.

Preparation Time: 10 minutes
Serves: 4

2 papaya, peeled, deseeded, and chilled
200ml (7fl oz) fat-free natural yogurt, chilled
3 bananas
juice of 1 orange
1–2 tbsp honey (optional)
fresh basil or mint leaves, to decorate (optional)

Slice 1 papaya and reserve to decorate. Place all the remaining ingredients, with the exception of the basil leaves, in a blender, and process into a smooth purée. Serve decorated with the reserved slices of fresh papaya and the basil leaves.

VARIATIONS

Kiwi Fruit and Passion Fruit Smoothie Replace the papaya with 4 peeled kiwi fruit and the pulp of 3 passion fruit. Blend the kiwi fruit smoothly with the yogurt, bananas, orange juice, and honey, if using, then stir in the passion fruit pulp. Decorate with a slice of orange.

Raspberry and Pear Smoothie Replace the papaya and bananas with 125g (4oz) raspberries and 3 ripe pears, peeled and cored. Replace the orange juice with the juice of half a lemon. Blend these ingredients with the yogurt and honey, if using. Decorate with raspberries and mint leaves.

BREAKFASTS

Breakfasts literally break the fast of the night, and are important for recharging the body and providing nutrients and long-term, sustained energy. These recipes include quick ideas for every day, and suggestions for more leisurely occasions.

EXOTIC DRIED FRUIT SALAD

THIS DELICIOUS, HIGH-FIBRE FRUIT SALAD SHOULD BE MADE THE
NIGHT BEFORE IT IS EATEN. SERVE IT WITH A SPOONFUL OF LOW-FAT
NATURAL YOGURT AND SLICES OF WHOLEMEAL OR GRANARY BREAD.
A SPRINKLING OF MUESLI ADDS A PLEASANT CRUNCH.

30g (1oz) dried pineapple, sliced into bite-sized pieces
30g (1oz) dried mango, sliced into bite-sized pieces
30g (1oz) dried, pitted cherries or cranberries
30g (1oz) dried prunes
350ml (12fl oz) unsweetened pineapple juice
juice of ½ lemon and ½ tsp grated zest
1–2 tbsp honey or sugar (optional)

1 Put the dried fruits in a large, non-corrosive bowl.

2 Put the pineapple juice, lemon juice and zest, and honey, if using,
in a small saucepan, and heat gently but do not boil. Pour the liquid
over the fruits. Leave to cool, cover, and refrigerate overnight.

APRICOT & DATE MUESLI

THIS IS A BALANCED AND ENERGY-PACKED MIXTURE OF DRIED FRUITS
AND HIGH-FIBRE CEREALS. I LIKE TO MAKE A LARGE QUANTITY OF
THIS MUESLI AND STORE IT IN AN AIRTIGHT CONTAINER.

150g (5oz) jumbo oats
150g (5oz) barley flakes
150g (5oz) oat bran
150g (5oz) wheat flakes
100g (3½oz) raisins
100g (3½oz) dried apricots, chopped
100g (3½oz) dried dates, chopped

Mix the cereals and dried fruits together in a large bowl. Transfer the
mixture to an airtight container, and store for up to 2 weeks.

PORRIDGE WITH SUMMER FRUITS

OATS HAVE AN IMPORTANT ROLE TO PLAY IN A HEALTHY
HEART DIET BECAUSE THEY ARE REPUTED TO LOWER CHOLESTEROL
LEVELS. THIS WARMING WINTER BREAKFAST IS ALSO DELICIOUS
SPRINKLED WITH FLAKED GRAINS.

750ml (1¼ pints) fat-free milk or water
6 tbsp jumbo oats
150g (5oz) berries, such as raspberries, strawberries, or blueberries

1 Bring the milk to a boil. Sprinkle the oats over the milk, and
stir well. Reduce the heat and simmer, stirring frequently, for
20–25 minutes, until thick and creamy.

2 Add the berries, reserving a few to decorate, and cook for
a further minute. Decorate with the reserved berries.

EACH SERVING PROVIDES:

○ Calories 160

○ Protein 10g

○ Carbohydrate 30g
Fibre 3g

○ Total Fat 3g
Saturated Fat 1g
Polyunsaturated Fat 1g
Monounsaturated Fat 1g

○ Cholesterol 8mg

○ Sodium 112mg

Preparation Time: 30 minutes
Serves: 4

MALTED MILLET PORRIDGE

MILLET IS ONE OF NATURE'S MOST NUTRITIONALLY BALANCED FOODS:
ABUNDANT IN VITAMINS AND MINERALS, IT IS ALSO HIGH IN FIBRE.
THIS PORRIDGE MAKES AN IDEAL START TO THE DAY.

500ml (17fl oz) fat-free milk or water
2 tbsp malt extract
6 tbsp millet flour
2–3 tbsp honey (optional)

1 In a small saucepan, bring the milk to a boil. Add the malt extract
and stir well until melted. Sprinkle with the millet flour and stir.

2 Reduce the heat and simmer, stirring frequently, for 20–25 minutes,
until thick and creamy. Serve drizzled with honey, if desired.

EACH SERVING PROVIDES:

○ Calories 140

○ Protein 6g

○ Carbohydrate 30g
Fibre 1g

○ Total Fat 1g
Saturated Fat <1g
Polyunsaturated Fat <1g
Monounsaturated Fat <1g

○ Cholesterol 5mg

○ Sodium 73mg

PREPARATION TIPS

Ground millet can be found
in health food shops. Coarse
cornmeal can also be used.

Preparation Time: 30 minutes
Serves: 4

EACH SERVING PROVIDES:

○ Calories 60

○ Protein 1g

○ Carbohydrate 15g
   Fibre 2g

○ Total Fat <0.5g
   Saturated Fat 0g
   Polyunsaturated Fat 0g
   Monounsaturated Fat 0g

○ Cholesterol 0mg

○ Sodium 5mg

Preparation Time: 5 minutes
Serves: 4

STRAWBERRY & MANGO SALAD

THIS WONDERFULLY REFRESHING, SWEET, AND VIBRANT SUMMER
BREAKFAST DISH IS EQUALLY DELICIOUS MADE WITH OTHER
COMBINATIONS OF FRESH, SEASONAL FRUITS. SERVE IT WITH A DOLLOP
OF LOW-FAT NATURAL YOGURT AND SLICES OF WHOLEMEAL TOAST.

juice of 1 orange
juice of ½ lemon
honey or sugar, to taste (optional)
1 large mango, peeled, stoned, and cubed
250g (8oz) strawberries, hulled and quartered

Place the orange juice, lemon juice, and honey, if using, in a bowl.
Add the mango and strawberries as they are prepared, and fold them
into the citrus liquid. Serve immediately.

EACH SERVING PROVIDES:

○ Calories 110

○ Protein 1g

○ Carbohydrate 18g
   Fibre 2g

○ Total Fat 4g
   Saturated Fat 0g
   Polyunsaturated Fat 1g
   Monounsaturated Fat 3g

○ Cholesterol 0mg

○ Sodium 162mg

Preparation Time: 15 minutes,
plus 2 hours marinating
Serves: 4

GRIDDLED SPICED PINEAPPLE

1 tbsp reduced salt soy sauce
1 tbsp molasses or soft, dark-brown sugar
½ tsp ground star anise
juice of ½ lemon
1 pineapple, peeled, cored, and sliced into
2.5cm (1in) rings
1 tbsp grapeseed or sunflower oil

1 In a large bowl, mix together the soy sauce, molasses, star anise,
and lemon juice. Add the pineapple and carefully turn the rings in the
marinade until coated. Leave to marinate for at least 2 hours.

2 Heat a lightly oiled griddle. Cook the pineapple for 3–4 minutes
on each side, until it starts to turn golden and blacken. Alternatively,
preheat the grill to high, brush the pineapple with the oil, and grill for
3–4 minutes on each side. Serve immediately.

✳ STAR INGREDIENT

Use basil regularly in cooking to boost intake of the antioxidants vitamin C and beta-carotene. Basil is both a tonic and calming to the nervous system.

EACH SERVING PROVIDES:

○ Calories 260

○ Protein 16g

○ Carbohydrate 39g
Fibre 3g

○ Total Fat 6g
Saturated Fat 3g
Polyunsaturated Fat 1g
Monounsaturated Fat 2g

○ Cholesterol 11mg

○ Sodium 421mg

Preparation Time: 30 minutes, plus 1 hour chilling, and 1–2 hours freezing
Serves: 4

LOW-FAT BREAKFAST SAUSAGES

THESE DELICIOUS VEGETARIAN SAUSAGES CAN ALSO BE
SERVED AS A STARTER, LIGHT LUNCH, OR SUPPER DISH. SERVE THEM
WITH GRILLED TOMATOES, MUSHROOMS, AND SLICES OF
WHOLEMEAL BREAD OR TOAST.

150g (5oz) half-fat mozzarella, coarsely grated
200g (7oz) fresh breadcrumbs
*30g (1oz) sun-dried tomatoes, rehydrated in boiling water
for 30 minutes, and chopped*
4 spring onions, with green tops, chopped
2 tbsp chopped fresh parsley
2 tbsp chopped fresh basil
2 tsp lemon juice, plus ¼ tsp grated zest
freshly ground black pepper, to taste
2 large egg whites
2 tbsp water or fat-free milk
75–100g (3–3½oz) dried breadcrumbs, for coating

1 Place the mozzarella, fresh breadcrumbs, tomatoes, spring onions, herbs, and lemon juice and zest in a bowl. Season, then add the white of 1 egg, and mix well. Refrigerate the mixture for about an hour.

2 Shape the mixture into short sausages. Beat the remaining egg white with the water in a shallow bowl. Dip each sausage in the egg mixture, then roll in the breadcrumbs until coated.

3 Freeze the sausages for 1–2 hours, or until quite firm. Preheat the grill to high. Grill the sausages for 5–8 minutes, turning occasionally, until firm and browned.

CARROT & COURGETTE GRIDDLE CAKES

IRON GRIDDLES ARE IDEAL FOR LOW-FAT COOKING. FOR THESE LIGHT FRITTERS, A CAST-IRON GRIDDLE WITH A THICK BASE, A FLAT SURFACE, AND A NON-STICK FINISH IS PREFERABLE.

2 carrots, finely grated
4 courgettes, finely grated
4 spring onions, finely chopped
3 tbsp chopped fresh flat-leaf parsley
1 tbsp olive oil, plus extra for greasing
1 tsp caraway seeds, lightly toasted in a dry frying pan,
and crushed (optional)
2 egg whites
3–4 tbsp matzo meal or dry breadcrumbs
salt and freshly ground black pepper, to taste

1 Place the carrots and courgettes in a large bowl. Cover with boiling water, stir, and leave to stand for 1–2 minutes, until slightly softened.

2 Drain the carrots and courgettes, leave them to cool slightly, then squeeze dry in a tea towel. Return the vegetables to the bowl, then add the remaining ingredients, and mix well. Cover, then refrigerate for 20–30 minutes to allow the mixture to settle.

3 Heat a lightly oiled griddle. Place large tablespoons of the vegetable mixture on the hot griddle, and flatten each spoonful to make a small cake, about 1.5cm (¾in) thick. Cook the griddle cakes for 3–4 minutes on each side, until firm and golden. (You will probably have to cook the cakes in batches.)

VARIATION

Carrot and Cucumber Griddle Cakes Replace the courgettes with 1 large cucumber, deseeded and finely grated.

★ STAR INGREDIENT
Carrots are probably the best-known source of beta-carotene, the antioxidant that fights free radicals, thus preventing cell damage.

EACH SERVING PROVIDES:

○ Calories 125

○ Protein 5g

○ Carbohydrate 16g
 Fibre 3g

○ Total Fat 5g
 Saturated Fat 1g
 Polyunsaturated Fat 1g
 Monounsaturated Fat 3g

○ Cholesterol 0mg

○ Sodium 51mg

SERVING TIP
The griddle cakes are delicious served with a spoonful of low-sugar jam.

Preparation Time: 20 minutes, plus 30 minutes resting
Serves: 4

SPICED FISH KEDGEREE

KEDGEREE TRADITIONALLY INCORPORATES SMOKED FISH,
WHICH IS HIGH IN SALT. THIS LOWER-SALT ALTERNATIVE IS MADE
WITH FRESH HADDOCK, WITH STAR ANISE GIVING THE DISH
A SMOKY FLAVOUR. SERVE IT WITH GRILLED TOMATOES.

juice of 1 lemon
1 tsp mild curry powder
1 tsp ground star anise
½ tsp ground turmeric
350g (11½oz) haddock fillets
750ml (1¼ pints) water
1 small lemon, sliced into thin rounds
1 bay leaf
10 peppercorns
1 large onion, finely chopped
200g (7oz) long-grain rice
3 tbsp chopped fresh parsley, plus sprigs to garnish
salt and freshly ground black pepper, to taste
lemon wedges, to garnish

1 Combine the lemon juice, curry powder, star anise, and turmeric, then spoon the mixture over the haddock. Turn the fish in the marinade to coat both sides. Cover, and refrigerate for at least 30 minutes.

2 Place the water, lemon slices, bay leaf, and peppercorns in a large frying pan and bring to a boil. Reduce the heat, and simmer for 10 minutes. Add the fish and marinade, then cook for a further 8–10 minutes, until the fish is tender. Lift out the fish, remove any skin and bones, then flake the flesh. Strain and reserve the liquid.

3 Place the onion in a saucepan with 5 tablespoons of the reserved liquid. Bring to a boil, cover, then simmer for 6 minutes. Add the rice and the remaining cooking liquid. Bring to a boil, reduce the heat and simmer, covered, for 20 minutes, or until the rice is tender. Add the fish and chopped parsley, and heat through. Season, and garnish with the parsley sprigs and the lemon wedges.

✱ STAR INGREDIENT

White fish such as haddock is an excellent source of low-fat protein, and also provides selenium, iodine, and vitamin E.

EACH SERVING PROVIDES:

○ Calories 270

○ Protein 21g

○ Carbohydrate 43g
  Fibre 1g

○ Total Fat 1g
  Saturated Fat <1g
  Polyunsaturated Fat <1g
  Monounsaturated Fat <1g

○ Cholesterol 32mg

○ Sodium 65mg

PREPARATION TIP

For a vegetarian version, use 350g (11½oz) smoked or plain tofu, cubed, instead of the fish. Add to the cooked rice in step 3.

Preparation Time: 50 minutes, plus 30 minutes marinating
Serves: 4

CHERRY SOUP

WHAT COULD BE BETTER ON A HOT SUMMER'S DAY THAN THIS
CHILLED, VIBRANT SOUP? CHERRIES ARE REPUTED TO MAINTAIN
A HEALTHY HEART AND PROMOTE GENERAL GOOD HEALTH. SERVE
THE SOUP WITH SLICES OF LIGHTLY TOASTED BREAD.

✶ **STAR INGREDIENT**
Cherries provide valuable
amounts of vitamin C, an
antioxidant that may help to
protect against heart disease.

EACH SERVING PROVIDES:

○ Calories 90

○ Protein 2g

○ Carbohydrate 20g
  Fibre 1g

○ Total Fat <1g
  Saturated Fat 0g
  Polyunsaturated Fat <1g
  Monounsaturated Fat <1g

○ Cholesterol 0mg

○ Sodium 126mg

PREPARATION TIP
Avoid buying stock cubes that
are high in salt. Homemade
stocks or good-quality shop-
bought ones are preferable.

Preparation Time: 25 minutes,
plus 1 hour chilling
Serves: 4

500g (1lb) cherries, pitted and coarsely chopped
500ml (17fl oz) chicken or vegetable stock
(see pages 118–19), or water
2 tbsp honey or sugar
½ cinnamon stick
2 tsp cornflour
2 tbsp lemon juice
zest of 1 lemon, cut into fine strips,
plus extra, to garnish (optional)
4 tbsp fat-free fromage frais or natural yogurt

1 Place the cherries in a large, stainless steel or enamel saucepan.
Add the stock, honey, and cinnamon. Bring to a boil, then reduce the
heat and simmer for 15 minutes, or until the cherries have softened.

2 Mix the cornflour with the lemon juice, and stir into the soup.
Simmer for a few more minutes until slightly thickened. Add the
lemon zest, and remove from the heat. Leave to cool, then chill for
1 hour. Divide the soup between 4 bowls and place a tablespoon of
fromage frais on top of each portion. Garnish with strips of lemon
zest, if using, before serving.

SOUPS *Nutritious, sustaining, and incredibly*
versatile, homemade soups are the perfect food for a healthy heart and body.
Served with a chunk of good-quality bread (preferably wholemeal) and a
fresh green or mixed salad, a soup makes a light yet satisfying low-fat meal.

EACH SERVING PROVIDES:

○ Calories 140

○ Protein 3g

○ Carbohydrate 23g
Fibre 2g

○ Total Fat 5g
Saturated Fat <1g
Polyunsaturated Fat <1g
Monounsaturated Fat 3g

○ Cholesterol 0mg

○ Sodium 13mg

BUYING TIP

Whenever possible use fresh tomatoes such as Italian plum or beef varieties. Salad tomatoes tend to be too watery and lack the intensity of flavour needed for cooking.

Preparation Time: 60 minutes
Serves: 4

WINTER TOMATO SOUP

TRY THIS LOW-FAT VERSION OF AN OLD FAVOURITE. IT IS CREAMY, SWEET-SOUR, AND WARMING, AND AS WELL AS TASTING GOOD, IT CONTAINS A VALUABLE COMBINATION OF VITAMINS AND MINERALS. SERVE THIS SOUP WITH A CHUNK OF WHOLEMEAL BREAD.

1 onion, finely chopped
3 cloves garlic, finely chopped
2 celery sticks, finely chopped
juice and grated zest of 1 orange
1 tbsp olive oil
500g (1lb) tomatoes, skinned, deseeded,
and finely chopped
350ml (12fl oz) fresh orange juice
500ml (17fl oz) chicken or vegetable stock
(see pages 118–19)
2 tbsp pudding rice
freshly grated nutmeg, to taste
2–3 tbsp lemon juice, to taste
salt and freshly ground black pepper, to taste
chopped fresh basil, to garnish

1 Place the onion, garlic, celery, orange juice, and zest in a large saucepan. Cook for 5 minutes over a medium heat, or until the orange juice has evaporated. Stir in the oil and cook for a further 4–5 minutes, until the onion has softened and started to brown.

2 Add 400g (13oz) of the tomatoes, the fresh orange juice, stock, and rice. Bring to a boil, then reduce the heat, and simmer for about 35–40 minutes, until the soup has reduced and thickened. Add the nutmeg, lemon juice, and the remaining tomatoes, and heat through. Season, and garnish with the basil leaves before serving.

VARIATION

Summer Tomato Soup Omit the pudding rice, and cook the liquid as in step 2, above, for 25 minutes. Stir in the nutmeg, lemon juice, and the remaining tomatoes and heat through. Season and leave to cool, then refrigerate for at least 2 hours. Serve the soup chilled, garnished with the chopped basil.

MUSHROOM & BARLEY SOUP

ALTHOUGH BARLEY IS PROBABLY THE MOST ANCIENT CULTIVATED CEREAL CROP, IT IS OFTEN OVERLOOKED IN THE DIET. YET THIS NUTRITIOUS GRAIN IS REPUTED TO LOWER BLOOD-CHOLESTEROL LEVELS, AND MAKES A WONDERFULLY HEARTY, SATISFYING SOUP.

✷ STAR INGREDIENT

A regular intake of high-fibre grains, such as barley, has been linked to a reduced risk of heart disease, high blood pressure, and certain cancers.

EACH SERVING PROVIDES:

○ Calories 120

○ Protein 2g

○ Carbohydrate 20g
   Fibre 1g

○ Total Fat 4g
   Saturated Fat <1g
   Polyunsaturated Fat <1g
   Monounsaturated Fat 3g

○ Cholesterol 0mg

○ Sodium 198mg

PREPARATION TIP

Soak the barley for 2 hours in cold water before use to reduce the cooking time by half.

Preparation Time: 1 hour, 25 minutes
Serves: 4

---

1 tbsp olive oil or half-fat butter
*1 onion, chopped, or the white part
of 2 leeks, finely chopped*
*60g (2oz) pearl barley, soaked in cold water
for 2 hours, and drained*
*1 litre (1¾ pints) vegetable stock (see page 118),
skimmed milk, or water*
*20g (¾oz) dried porcini mushrooms, soaked
for 30 minutes in a little hot water*
1 bay leaf
1 large carrot, coarsely grated
salt and freshly ground black pepper, to taste

1 Heat the oil in a heavy-based saucepan, then add the onion. Cover, and cook over a medium heat for 5 minutes, or until the onion has softened.

2 Add the barley and cook for a further 1–2 minutes, until the barley is coated in the onion mixture. Add the stock, rehydrated mushrooms, together with their strained soaking liquid, and bay leaf. Bring to a boil, then reduce the heat and simmer for 1 hour, or until the barley is tender.

3 Add the carrot and continue to simmer the soup for 5–6 minutes, until the carrot is tender. Season before serving.

VARIATION

Smoky Mushroom and Barley Soup Add 50g (1½oz) smoked, dry-cured ham, cut into cubes and fat removed, with the carrot in step 3, above. (To remove the excess salt in the ham, blanch it first for 5 minutes in boiling water, then drain and rinse.)

MEDITERRANEAN BEAN SOUP

THIS IS A WARMING, FILLING SOUP THAT IS PACKED WITH A NUTRITIOUS

COMBINATION OF VEGETABLES, GRAINS, AND BEANS. SERVE IT WITH

CHUNKS OF ITALIAN-STYLE BREAD. BORLOTTI OR CANNELLINI BEANS

CAN BE USED INSTEAD OF THE BUTTER BEANS.

1 tbsp olive oil
1 large onion, chopped
3 cloves garlic, finely chopped
2 celery sticks, finely chopped
1 large carrot, finely chopped
1 litre (1¾ pints) chicken or vegetable stock
(see pages 118–19)
2 tbsp pearl barley, soaked in cold water
for 2 hours, and drained
150g (5oz) plum tomatoes, skinned,
deseeded, and chopped
200g (7oz) canned butter beans in water
small bunch of fresh parsley,
coarsely chopped
salt and freshly ground black pepper, to taste

1 Heat the oil in a large saucepan. Add the onion, garlic, celery, and carrot, then sauté over a medium heat for 5–8 minutes, until the onion has softened and browned. If the mixture becomes too dry, add 1–2 tablespoons of water.

2 Add the stock and barley. Bring to a boil, then reduce the heat, cover, and simmer for 1 hour, or until the barley is tender. Add the tomatoes, beans, and parsley, reserving a little of the herb to garnish. Simmer for a further 5 minutes, or until heated through. Season, and serve garnished with the reserved parsley.

★ STAR INGREDIENT

Beans provide significant amounts of soluble fibre, which may reduce cholesterol levels if eaten on a regular basis. They are also high in iron, folate, and potassium.

EACH SERVING PROVIDES:

○ Calories 210

○ Protein 16g

○ Carbohydrate 27g
   Fibre 6g

○ Total Fat 5g
   Saturated Fat 1g
   Polyunsaturated Fat 1g
   Monounsaturated Fat 3g

○ Cholesterol 0mg

○ Sodium 264mg

PREPARATION TIP

If using dried butter beans, soak 100g (3½oz) beans in cold water overnight, then drain and rinse. Cover with cold water in a saucepan and bring to a boil. Cover, reduce the heat, and simmer for 1–1½ hours, until tender. Add to the soup in step 2, with the tomatoes.

Preparation Time: 1 hour, 25 minutes
Serves: 4

LENTIL & CORIANDER SOUP

THIS CREAMY, LEMONY, SUBSTANTIAL SOUP FORMS A MEAL IN ITSELF
WHEN IT IS ACCOMPANIED BY NAAN OR OTHER, SIMILAR FLAT
BREADS. LENTILS ARE ESPECIALLY GOOD FOR THE HEART, AS THEY
PROVIDE BOTH FIBRE AND MINERALS.

✷ STAR INGREDIENT
Fresh herbs such as coriander
are an often overlooked source
of vitamin C. This antioxidant
may reduce the risk of heart
disease and strokes.

EACH SERVING PROVIDES:

○ Calories 230

○ Protein 19g

○ Carbohydrate 29g
   Fibre 3g

○ Total Fat 5g
   Saturated Fat 1g
   Polyunsaturated Fat 1g
   Monounsaturated Fat 3g

○ Cholesterol 0mg

○ Sodium 250mg

PREPARATION TIP
Puy, green, or brown lentils
can be used instead of the
red lentils.

Preparation Time: 50 minutes
Serves: 4

1 tbsp olive oil
1 onion, finely chopped
3 cloves garlic, finely chopped
1 large carrot, grated
small bunch of fresh coriander, chopped
125g (4oz) red lentils, rinsed
2 tbsp bulgar, rinsed
1 litre (1¾ pints) chicken or vegetable stock
(see pages 118–19)
juice and grated zest of 1 lemon
salt and freshly ground black pepper, to taste

1 Heat the oil in a large saucepan. Add the onion, garlic, carrot, and
coriander, reserving a little of the herb to garnish. Sauté over a medium
heat for 5–8 minutes, until the onion has softened and browned. If the
mixture becomes too dry, add 1–2 tablespoons of water.

2 Add the lentils and bulgar, stir well, then add the stock. Bring to
a boil, then reduce the heat, and simmer for 30 minutes, or until the
lentils are tender. Stir in the lemon juice and zest, then season. Serve
garnished with the reserved coriander.

VARIATIONS

Smoky Lentil and Coriander Soup Stir in 250g (8oz) smoked tofu,
cubed, about 10 minutes before the end of the specified cooking time.

Spicy Lentil and Coriander Soup Add 1–2 red chillies, deseeded and
chopped, with the onion in step 1, above. Stir in ¼ teaspoon ground
cumin with the lemon juice in step 2, above.

Thai Fish & Noodle Soup

THIS THAI-INSPIRED FISH SOUP IS SIMPLE TO MAKE, AND WHEN SERVED

WITH BREAD AND SALAD IT MAKES A DELICIOUS, LOW-FAT MEAL.

MONKFISH IS USED IN THIS VERSION, BUT OTHER FIRM, LEAN FISH,

SUCH AS HALIBUT OR SWORDFISH, ARE EQUALLY SUITABLE.

400g (13oz) monkfish fillet, cut into bite-sized cubes
juice of 1 lime, and 1 tsp grated zest
100g (3½oz) shallots, finely chopped
2 cloves garlic, finely chopped
1 carrot, finely shredded
2.5cm (1in) piece of fresh ginger, finely chopped
2 sticks of lemongrass, outer leaves discarded,
and inside finely chopped
1 small red chilli, deseeded and finely chopped
4 tbsp water
1 tbsp grapeseed oil
750ml (1¼ pints) fish stock (see page 118)
30g (1oz) rice noodles, broken into short lengths,
and soaked for 3 minutes in boiling water
fresh dill or coriander, to garnish

1 Place the monkfish in a dish. Spoon over the lime juice and half of the zest. Cover, and leave to marinate in the refrigerator for 30 minutes.

2 Place the shallots, garlic, carrot, ginger, lemongrass, and chilli in a large saucepan. Add the water, and bring to a boil. Reduce the heat, cover, and simmer, stirring occasionally, for 5 minutes, or until the water has evaporated. Add the oil and cook, stirring, until the vegetables have softened.

3 Add the stock, and return to the boil. Reduce the heat, skim away any froth, and simmer for about 20 minutes.

4 Add the fish and noodles to the soup, then simmer for 5–8 minutes, until the fish is tender. Stir in the lime juice and zest marinade. Garnish with the dill and reserved zest before serving.

---

* STAR INGREDIENT
Fresh fish is not only low in fat, but also provides high levels of protein in a healthy form.

EACH SERVING PROVIDES:

○ Calories 180

○ Protein 24g

○ Carbohydrate 10g
  Fibre 1g

○ Total Fat 5g
  Saturated Fat <1g
  Polyunsaturated Fat 3g
  Monounsaturated Fat <1g

○ Cholesterol 14mg

○ Sodium 198mg

PREPARATION TIP
To add a slightly smoky flavour to the monkfish, after marinating it, cook it for a few minutes on a hot, lightly greased griddle, until golden. Add the fish to the soup in step 4.

Preparation Time: 40 minutes, plus 30 minutes marinating
Serves: 4

ROASTED VEGETABLES WITH HERBS & GARLIC

ROASTING ENHANCES THE FLAVOUR OF FRESH VEGETABLES, MAKING

THEM SWEET AND AROMATIC. THIS DISH IS DELICIOUS SERVED

SIMPLY WITH PASTA OR BREAD AND A GREEN LEAF SALAD.

4 tbsp water or fresh orange juice
100g (3½oz) yellow or green courgettes, sliced into ribbons
1 red pepper, cored, deseeded, and sliced into ribbons
100g (3½oz) broccoli florets
5 shallots, quartered
3–4 cloves garlic, quartered
300g (10oz) vine cherry tomatoes
2 tbsp olive oil
2 tsp brown sugar
2 sprigs each of fresh rosemary and thyme
salt and freshly ground black pepper, to taste
fresh basil leaves, to garnish

1 Preheat the oven to 200°C/400°F/Gas 6. Pour the water over the courgettes, pepper, broccoli, shallots, and garlic in a baking tray. Cover with foil and bake for 25 minutes.

2 Increase the heat to 230°C/450°F/Gas 8. Remove the foil from the vegetables, then add the tomatoes, oil, sugar, herbs, and seasoning. Bake, turning the vegetables frequently, for 20–25 minutes, until they have browned and caramelized. Garnish with the basil before serving.

✷ STAR INGREDIENT

Red peppers are a good source of beta-carotene and vitamin C. These antioxidants are reputed to reduce the risk of heart disease.

EACH SERVING PROVIDES:

○ Calories 120

○ Protein 3g

○ Carbohydrate 9g
Fibre 2g

○ Total Fat 8g
Saturated Fat 1g
Polyunsaturated Fat 1g
Monounsaturated Fat 6g

○ Cholesterol 0mg

○ Sodium 15mg

SERVING TIPS

This dish is delicious cold and will keep in the refrigerator for up to 2 days. Serve it as an accompaniment to meat or fish.

Preparation Time: 55 minutes
Serves: 4

LIGHT MEALS

This eclectic range of dishes does not rely on excessive amounts of meat and fish to give substance, but is based on healthy and delicious vegetables, beans, and starchy carbohydrates, including bread, rice, bulgar, and pasta.

MY FAVOURITE SANDWICH

THIS SANDWICH FEATURES A HEALTHY COMBINATION OF TOMATOES,
ONIONS, AND PARSLEY, WHICH ARE ALL BELIEVED TO BENEFIT
THE HEART. I SOMETIMES ADD A LARGE, THINLY SLICED CLOVE OF
GARLIC, WHICH I LAY OVER THE TOMATOES.

3 thick slices of beef tomato or slicing tomato
½ tsp sugar
juice of ½ lemon
1–2 tsp olive oil
2 thick slices of wholegrain bread, lightly toasted
½ small red onion, sliced into thin rings
*handful of fresh flat-leaf parsley or basil,
stems included*
salt and freshly ground black pepper, to taste

1 Heat the grill to high, and line the grill pan with foil. Sprinkle the tomato slices with the sugar, and grill them on one side for 4–5 minutes, until softened and starting to brown.

2 Mix together the lemon juice and oil, then spoon this over a slice of the toasted bread. Arrange the tomatoes on the bread, and top with the onion and parsley. Season, cover with the other slice of toasted bread, and press down well before serving.

VARIATION

Aubergine Sandwich Substitute 3 slices of aubergine for the tomato. Brush each slice with 1 tsp olive oil, then cook under a hot grill for 4–5 minutes on each side, until softened and starting to brown. Replace the oil with ½ clove of crushed garlic and mix it with the lemon juice. Pour this over a slice of the toasted bread. Lay the aubergine slices on top of the bread and top with the onion and parsley. Season and cover with the other slice of toasted bread.

✳ STAR INGREDIENT
A good-quality wholegrain bread will boost your fibre intake and help to prevent constipation.

EACH SERVING PROVIDES:

○ Calories 270

○ Protein 9g

○ Carbohydrate 44g
Fibre 7g

○ Total Fat 7g
Saturated Fat 1g
Polyunsaturated Fat 2g
Monounsaturated Fat 4g

○ Cholesterol 0mg

○ Sodium 455mg

PREPARATION TIP
This sandwich improves in flavour if made an hour before serving. Wrap in cling film and refrigerate.

Preparation Time: 10 minutes
Serves: 1

STEAMED DAHL DUMPLINGS WITH YOGURT SAUCE

THESE FLUFFY DUMPLINGS ARE SURPRISINGLY LOW IN FAT, AND MAKE A
NUTRITIOUS, LIGHT MEAL OR STARTER. SERVE THEM WITH A MIXED
LEAF SALAD AND CHAPATTI OR OTHER, SIMILAR FLAT BREAD.

*75g (3oz) dried mung beans, soaked overnight,
rinsed, and drained*
*50g (1¾oz) dried chick-peas, soaked overnight,
rinsed, and drained*
2 egg whites
1 red chilli, deseeded and finely chopped
3–4 tbsp chopped fresh coriander
½ tsp cumin seeds, roasted in a dry frying pan
1 tsp baking powder
salt and freshly ground black pepper, to taste

FOR THE SAUCE
250ml (8fl oz) fat-free natural yogurt
juice of 1 lemon and ½ tsp finely grated zest
*2 tbsp chopped fresh coriander or mint,
plus extra, to garnish*

1 Place the mung beans, chick-peas, and egg whites in a food processor, and process until smooth. Add the chilli, coriander, cumin, baking powder, and seasoning, then process until the mixture forms a batter-like consistency. (If the mixture is too soft, add a little flour.)

2 Line the bottom of a steamer with muslin or baking parchment. If using the latter, pierce a few holes with a thin skewer to allow the steam to penetrate. Form dumplings from tablespoonfuls of the batter mixture and place them in the steamer. Cover, and cook them for about 10 minutes, or until just firm. (You may have to cook them in batches.)

3 To make the sauce, mix together all the ingredients, then pour over the warm dumplings. Leave the sauce to soak into the dumplings for about 15 minutes. Serve either chilled or at room temperature, sprinkled with the remaining coriander.

★ STAR INGREDIENT
Beans are low in fat and provide valuable amounts of soluble fibre. This has been shown to help reduce cholesterol levels in the blood.

EACH SERVING PROVIDES:

○ Calories 130

○ Protein 12g

○ Carbohydrate 20g
Fibre 1g

○ Total Fat 1g
Saturated Fat <1g
Polyunsaturated Fat <1g
Monounsaturated Fat 0g

○ Cholesterol 2mg

○ Sodium 205mg

PREPARATION TIP
These dumplings do not keep well and are best eaten soon after cooking.

Preparation Time: 20 minutes, plus 15 minutes resting
Serves: 4

FRESH VEGETABLE PATTIES

EACH SERVING PROVIDES:

- Calories 95
- Protein 5g
- Carbohydrate 15g
  Fibre 2g
- Total Fat 3g
  Saturated Fat <1g
  Polyunsaturated Fat <1g
  Monounsaturated Fat <1g
- Cholesterol 0mg
- Sodium 160mg

Preparation Time: 15 minutes,
plus 20 minutes chilling
Serves: 4

100g (3½oz) broccoli florets
100g (3½oz) carrots, chopped
4 spring onions, chopped
2 egg whites
4–5 tbsp flour

1 tsp baking powder
3–4 tbsp chopped fresh parsley or mint
salt and freshly ground black pepper,
to taste
1 tbsp oil, for greasing

1 Place the vegetables in a food processor, then process until finely chopped. Add the egg whites and blend, then mix in the remaining ingredients, except the oil. Cover, and refrigerate for 20 minutes.

2 Heat a lightly oiled griddle. Place tablespoonfuls of the mixture on the griddle, and with a small spatula spread into round patties. Cook the patties for about 3 minutes on each side, until golden.

BULGAR PILAFF WITH SPINACH

BULGAR IS PROBABLY ONE OF THE MOST ANCIENT "FAST FOODS".

IT IS EASY TO PREPARE, AND AN EXCELLENT AND NUTRITIOUS

ALTERNATIVE TO RICE OR COUSCOUS.

EACH SERVING PROVIDES:

- Calories 330
- Protein 10g
- Carbohydrate 51g
  Fibre 2g
- Total Fat 10g
  Saturated Fat 1g
  Polyunsaturated Fat 2g
  Monounsaturated Fat 6g
- Cholesterol 0mg
- Sodium 180mg

Preparation Time: 35 minutes,
plus 5 minutes standing
Serves: 4

2 tbsp olive oil
1 small onion, chopped
250g (8oz) bulgar
600ml (1 pint) boiling water
500g (1lb) spinach, coarsely chopped
salt and freshly ground black pepper, to taste
juice of 1 lemon

1 Heat the oil in a frying pan, then add the onion, and sauté for 5 minutes, until softened. Add the bulgar and fry, stirring frequently, for 5 minutes, or until the grains look toasted.

2 Add the water and bring to a boil, then reduce the heat. Cover, and simmer for 15–20 minutes, until the water has been absorbed.

3 Steam the spinach for 2 minutes, or until wilted, then add it to the bulgar mixture. Season, then add the lemon juice. Cover, and leave the mixture to stand for 5 minutes before serving.

QUICK TOMATO & FRESH HERB PILAFF

THIS IS A VARIATION OF THE CLASSIC MIDDLE EASTERN DISH
TABBOULEH. BULGAR WHEAT OR COUSCOUS CAN BE USED AS
A NUTRITIOUS ALTERNATIVE TO THE RICE.

4 tomatoes, diced
2 small cucumbers, diced
4 spring onions, finely chopped
1 clove garlic, chopped
1 chilli, deseeded and finely chopped
juice of 1 lemon, or to taste
small bunch of fresh mint or
flat-leaf parsley leaves, chopped
2 tbsp olive oil
salt and freshly ground black pepper, to taste
200g (7oz) basmati rice
400ml (14fl oz) water

1 Combine the tomatoes, cucumbers, spring onions, garlic, chilli, lemon juice, herbs, seasoning, and half the oil in a bowl. Cover and leave to marinate for at least 1 hour to allow the flavours to develop.

2 Heat the remaining oil in a large, heavy-based saucepan. Add the rice, and fry over a high heat, stirring constantly, for 3–4 minutes, until the rice starts to colour.

3 Add the water and bring to a rapid boil. Reduce the heat to minimum, cover, and simmer for 15 minutes, or until the rice is tender and the water has been absorbed. Leave the rice to stand for 5 minutes.

4 To serve, arrange the marinated tomato and cucumber salad on top of the cooked rice. Alternatively, mix the salad into the rice, and gently heat through before serving.

EACH SERVING PROVIDES:

- Calories 270
- Protein 5g
- Carbohydrate 44g
  Fibre 1g
- Total Fat 8g
  Saturated Fat 1g
  Polyunsaturated Fat 1g
  Monounsaturated Fat 6g
- Cholesterol 0mg
- Sodium 9mg

PREPARATION TIPS

Brown rice can be used instead of white. Add a little extra water and cook for 30–40 minutes, until tender. To reduce the fat content of the dish, steam or boil the rice rather than frying it.

Preparation Time: 25 minutes, plus 1 hour marinating and 5 minutes standing
Serves: 4

PUMPKIN RISOTTO

FOR A DECORATIVE DINNER PARTY DISH, SERVE THIS LIGHT AND FRAGRANT RISOTTO IN A SCOOPED-OUT PUMPKIN SHELL. RING THE CHANGES BY USING BUTTERNUT SQUASH, PATTY PANS, OR COURGETTES AND ADDING A TEASPOON OF CINNAMON OR NUTMEG.

*500g (1lb) pumpkin, deseeded,
and cut into small cubes*
2 tbsp olive oil
1 onion, finely chopped
250g (8oz) arborio rice
*50g (1¾oz) sultanas, soaked in hot water
for 20 minutes*
*1 litre (1¾ pints) hot chicken or vegetable stock
(see pages 118–19)*
juice and grated zest of 1 lemon
salt and freshly ground black pepper, to taste
3 tbsp chopped fresh mint or flat-leaf parsley
*2 tbsp pumpkin seeds, lightly roasted
in a dry frying pan (optional)*

1 Steam the pumpkin for 8–10 minutes, until just tender. Meanwhile, heat the oil in a large saucepan. Add the onion and fry for 4–5 minutes, until softened. Stir in the rice and cook for 2 minutes, until the rice is coated in the oil. Mix in the sultanas.

2 Add about a third of the stock, reduce the heat, and simmer for 5–6 minutes, stirring frequently, until the liquid has been absorbed. Add half of the remaining stock and cook, stirring frequently, until the liquid has been absorbed.

3 Add the remaining stock and the pumpkin, then simmer for a further 5–6 minutes, until the rice is creamy and tender but still retains a slight bite. Stir in the lemon juice, half of the zest, and the seasoning.

4 Sprinkle the mint, pumpkin seeds, if using, and remaining lemon zest over the top of the risotto before serving.

✱ **STAR INGREDIENT**

Pumpkin is rich in vitamin C and beta-carotene. Eating foods rich in these antioxidants on a regular basis is thought to lower the risk of heart disease and strokes.

EACH SERVING PROVIDES:

○ Calories 360

○ Protein 7g

○ Carbohydrate 61g
    Fibre 2g

○ Total Fat 9g
    Saturated Fat 1g
    Polyunsaturated Fat 1g
    Monounsaturated Fat 6g

○ Cholesterol 0mg

○ Sodium 230mg

SERVING TIP

If you wish to serve the risotto in pumpkin shells, scoop out the seeds and most of the flesh from 4 small pumpkins before filling them with the risotto.

Preparation Time: 40 minutes
Serves: 4

✻ STAR INGREDIENT
Apples are rich in soluble fibre
and pectin, both of which may
help to lower cholesterol levels
in the blood.

EACH SERVING PROVIDES:

○ Calories 370

○ Protein 8g

○ Carbohydrate 66g
Fibre 4g

○ Total Fat 10g
Saturated Fat 2g
Polyunsaturated Fat 2g
Monounsaturated Fat 6g

○ Cholesterol 0mg

○ Sodium 132mg

PREPARATION TIP
To bake: preheat the oven to
200°C/400°F/Gas 6. Follow
step 1, then add the apple and
peas and increase the stock or
water to 600ml (1 pint). Place
the mixture in an ovenproof
dish and bake, covered, for
15 minutes. Remove the lid and
bake for a further 20 minutes,
until the liquid has been
absorbed and the rice is tender.

Preparation Time: 50 minutes,
plus 5 minutes standing
Serves: 4

RISI-BIZI

THIS SIMPLIFIED VERSION OF RISOTTO IS DELICIOUS TOPPED

WITH A SPOONFUL OF NATURAL YOGURT. FOR A MORE SUBSTANTIAL

MAIN COURSE, ADD SLIVERS OF SKINNED, ROASTED, OR

GRILLED CHICKEN BREAST OR FISH.

2 tbsp olive oil
1 onion, finely chopped
2 cloves garlic, finely chopped
2 carrots, grated
250g (8oz) long-grain rice
1 small dessert apple, unpeeled, cored,
and finely chopped
125g (4oz) shelled garden or frozen peas
500ml (17fl oz) vegetable stock (see page 118) or water
a few sprigs of fresh thyme (optional)
1 tsp finely grated lemon zest (optional)
salt and freshly ground black pepper, to taste

1 Heat the oil in a heavy-based saucepan with a lid. Add the onion,
garlic, and carrots, then fry for 8–10 minutes, until browned. Add the
rice and fry, stirring, for 1 minute, until it is coated in the oil mixture.

2 Add the apple, peas, and stock. Bring to a boil, then reduce the
heat to minimum and cover the pan with a tight-fitting lid. Simmer
gently for about 20–25 minutes, until the rice is tender and the
water has been absorbed.

3 Add the thyme and lemon zest, if using, and season. Fluff up the rice
with a fork, and leave to stand, covered, for 5 minutes before serving.

VARIATION
Pineapple Risi-bizi Replace the apples with 150g (5oz) fresh pineapple,
peeled, cored and chopped, and 30g (1oz) sultanas, soaked in hot water
for 20 minutes.

ORIENTAL MUSHROOM RISOTTO

INCORPORATING CREAMY ITALIAN ARBORIO RICE AND ORIENTAL

SHIITAKE MUSHROOMS, THIS RECIPE COMBINES THE FLAVOURS OF EAST

AND WEST. MUSHROOMS CONTAIN NUMEROUS VITAMINS,

AND HAVE ANTIVIRAL PROPERTIES.

★ STAR INGREDIENT

Shiitake and other oriental mushrooms have been found to lower levels of harmful cholesterol in the body.

EACH SERVING PROVIDES:

○ Calories 430

○ Protein 15g

○ Carbohydrate 77g
  Fibre 1g

○ Total Fat 9g
  Saturated Fat 1g
  Polyunsaturated Fat 5g
  Monounsaturated Fat 2g

○ Cholesterol 0mg

○ Sodium 180mg

PREPARATION TIP

If you cannot find fresh shiitake mushrooms, use dried instead. Rehydrate 30g (1oz) dried mushrooms in hot water for 30 minutes. Remove and discard the stems and use the mushrooms as specified.

Preparation Time: 40 minutes
Serves: 4

2 tbsp sunflower oil
1 small onion, finely chopped
2 cloves garlic, chopped
1.5cm (⅗in) piece fresh ginger, finely shredded
125g (4oz) shiitake mushrooms, stems discarded,
and caps thickly sliced
125g (4oz) field mushrooms, sliced
250ml (8fl oz) dry white wine
250g (8oz) arborio rice
750ml (1¼ pints) hot chicken or vegetable stock
(see pages 118–19)
salt and freshly ground black pepper, to taste
1 tbsp chopped fresh thyme or
2 tbsp chopped fresh flat-leaf parsley
shavings of Parmesan, to garnish (optional)

1 Heat the oil in a large, heavy-based saucepan, then add the onion, garlic, and ginger. Fry for 4–5 minutes, until the onion starts to brown.

2 Add all the mushrooms and sauté for 4–5 minutes, until the mushrooms soften and start to exude liquid. Add the white wine and bring to a boil. Reduce the heat and simmer, uncovered, for 10 minutes, or until most of the liquid has evaporated.

3 Add the rice, and stir for about 1 minute, or until the rice is coated in the mushroom mixture. Add about a third of the stock and simmer for 5–6 minutes, stirring occasionally, until the liquid has been absorbed. Add half of the remaining stock and cook, stirring frequently, until the liquid has been absorbed.

4 Add the remaining stock and cook for a further 5–6 minutes, until the rice is creamy and tender but still firm to the bite. Season, then sprinkle with the thyme and Parmesan, if using, before serving.

RICH AUBERGINE & TOMATO PASTA

PASTA IS A CONVENIENT AND VERSATILE LOW-FAT FOOD. CHOOSE FROM
THE WIDE RANGE OF PASTA SHAPES NOW AVAILABLE TO ACCOMPANY
THE RICH, AROMATIC TOMATO SAUCE. SERVE THIS DISH WITH A SALAD.

EACH SERVING PROVIDES:

○ Calories 380

○ Protein 12g

○ Carbohydrate 67g
Fibre 2g

○ Total Fat 10g
Saturated Fat 1g
Polyunsaturated Fat 2g
Monounsaturated Fat 6g

○ Cholesterol 0mg

○ Sodium 287mg

PREPARATION TIP

Avoid peeling the aubergine
because the skin helps to retain
the shape of the cubes and
enhances the appearance of
the dish.

Preparation Time: 45 minutes
Serves: 4

2 tbsp olive oil
1 large onion, chopped
4 cloves garlic, chopped
250g (8oz) aubergine, cut into 1cm (½in) cubes
1 tbsp reduced salt soy sauce
400g (13oz) canned tomatoes
250g (8oz) plum tomatoes, skinned, deseeded,
and chopped
2 tbsp chopped fresh thyme or oregano
300g (10oz) pasta shapes, such as riccioli,
fusilli, or conchiglie
freshly ground black pepper, to taste
handful of chopped fresh flat-leaf parsley,
to garnish

1 Heat the oil in a large, heavy-based saucepan, then add the onion
and garlic. Fry for 5–8 minutes, until the onion has softened. Add the
aubergine and fry for 5 minutes, or until it has softened slightly. If the
mixture becomes too dry, add 1–2 tablespoons of water.

2 Add the soy sauce and cook for 1–2 minutes, stirring. Add the
canned tomatoes, breaking down any large lumps with the back of a
spoon. Cover, and cook for about 20 minutes, or until the aubergine
is soft and tender. Add the fresh tomatoes and thyme, and simmer for
a further 2 minutes to heat through.

3 While the sauce is cooking, prepare the pasta following the
manufacturer's instructions. Season the sauce, and serve with the pasta.
Sprinkle with the parsley before serving.

Fresh Herb & Cottage Cheese Pasta

VIRTUALLY FAT-FREE COTTAGE CHEESE IS A USEFUL INGREDIENT IN THE

HEALTHY HEART KITCHEN. TANGY, CREAMY, AND VERSATILE, IT ALSO

ADDS TEXTURE AND MOISTURE TO SALADS AND SANDWICHES.

300g (10oz) tagliatelle
1 tbsp olive oil
250g (8oz) virtually fat-free cottage cheese
4 spring onions, finely chopped
small bunch of fresh flat-leaf parsley,
coarsely chopped
salt and freshly ground black pepper, to taste

1 Cook the pasta following the manufacturer's instructions, then drain.

2 Heat the oil in a saucepan, then add the pasta, tossing until it is coated in the oil. Add the remaining ingredients, reserving a little of the parsley to garnish, and mix well. Heat through and serve sprinkled with the reserved parsley.

Variation

Fresh Herb and Garlic Pasta Replace the cottage cheese with a crushed clove of garlic and 1 tablespoon of olive oil.

✴ STAR INGREDIENT

Spring onions have both cleansing and healing properties, and may help to reduce cholesterol levels in the blood.

EACH SERVING PROVIDES:

○ Calories 340

○ Protein 18g

○ Carbohydrate 58g
  Fibre 3g

○ Total Fat 6g
  Saturated Fat 1g
  Polyunsaturated Fat 1g
  Monounsaturated Fat 3g

○ Cholesterol 3mg

○ Sodium 243mg

PREPARATION TIP

This dish is equally delicious served cold. Stir the cheese and the rest of the ingredients into the warm pasta. Leave to cool, then chill before serving.

Preparation Time: 20 minutes
Serves: 4

TAGLIATELLE WITH TUNA SAUCE

VERSATILE AS WELL AS CONVENIENT, CANNED TUNA IS A USEFUL STORECUPBOARD STANDBY, BUT BE SURE TO BUY THE LOW-SALT VARIETY: LOOK FOR TUNA IN SPRING WATER RATHER THAN IN BRINE. SERVE THIS DISH WITH A GREEN SALAD.

2 tbsp olive oil
1 tsp fennel seeds (optional)
1 large onion, chopped
3 cloves garlic, chopped
500g (1lb) tomatoes, skinned, deseeded, and chopped
2 tbsp tomato purée, diluted in 100ml (3½fl oz) red
or white wine, stock
(see pages 118–19), or water
bouquet garni, made up of a few sprigs
of fresh thyme, fennel leaves, sprig of parsley,
and 2 strips of lemon zest
300g (10oz) tagliatelle
200g (7oz) canned tuna in spring water,
drained and flaked
2 tsp capers, rinsed and coarsely chopped
(left whole if small)
3 tbsp chopped fresh parsley or
2 tbsp fresh lemon thyme or tarragon
salt and freshly ground black pepper, to taste

1 Heat the oil in a large frying pan. Add the fennel seeds, if using, and fry for 2–3 minutes, or until they release a spicy aroma. Add the onion and garlic, then cook for 5 minutes, or until the onion has softened. If the mixture becomes too dry, add 1–2 tablespoons of water.

2 Add the tomatoes, the tomato purée mixture, and the bouquet garni. Bring to a boil, reduce the heat, and simmer for about 30 minutes, or until most of the liquid has evaporated.

3 Cook the pasta following the manufacturer's instructions, then drain.

4 Add the tuna, capers, and parsley to the tomato sauce. Season, and continue to cook for 2–3 minutes to allow the flavours to develop. Mix the sauce into the cooked tagliatelle before serving.

✱ STAR INGREDIENT
Tomatoes are a good source
of vitamins E and C, and also
contain the antioxidant
lycopene, which may protect
against heart disease.

EACH SERVING PROVIDES:

○ Calories 230

○ Protein 31g

○ Carbohydrate 6g
  Fibre 2g

○ Total Fat 9g
  Saturated Fat 1g
  Polyunsaturated Fat 1g
  Monounsaturated Fat 6g

○ Cholesterol 68mg

○ Sodium 159mg

PREPARATION TIP
Other fish, such as haddock,
halibut, or trout, can be used
instead of cod.

Preparation Time: 40 minutes,
plus 30 minutes marinating
Serves: 4

BAKED COD WITH TOMATO & PEPPER SALSA

BRIGHTLY COLOURED TOMATOES, PEPPERS, AND PARSLEY ADD TO THE

APPEARANCE AND NUTRITIONAL VALUE OF THIS EASY-TO-PREPARE DISH.

SERVE IT WITH A GREEN VEGETABLE SUCH AS FRENCH BEANS.

juice of 2 lemons, and grated zest of 1, plus extra, to garnish
4 cod or haddock steaks, each about 175g (6oz)
2 tbsp olive oil
salt and freshly ground black pepper, to taste

FOR THE SALSA
4 plum tomatoes, skinned, deseeded, and finely chopped
1 yellow or green pepper, cored, deseeded, and finely chopped
1 celery stick, finely chopped
1 onion, finely chopped
1–2 green chillies, deseeded and finely chopped
1 clove garlic, finely chopped
small bunch of fresh flat-leaf parsley, finely chopped

1 Place the lemon juice and zest in a shallow dish, then add the fish, turning once to coat both sides. Cover, and refrigerate for 30 minutes.

2 Mix together the salsa ingredients in a bowl, reserving some parsley.

3 Preheat the oven to 220°C/425°F/Gas 7. Brush a baking dish with a little of the oil, then arrange the fish on it. Spoon the salsa over the steaks and season. Sprinkle with the marinade and the remaining oil. Bake for 20 minutes, until tender. Garnish with lemon zest and parsley.

MAIN MEALS

This innovative and inspiring selection of recipes incorporates all the nutritional prerequisites necessary for a healthy heart and body. Serve them with fresh salads, steamed vegetables, or simple grain dishes.

✳ STAR INGREDIENT
Apples contain quercetin, which may protect against heart disease, as well as pectin, which is believed to help lower blood-cholesterol levels.

EACH SERVING PROVIDES:

○ Calories 295

○ Protein 39g

○ Carbohydrate 12g
Fibre 3g

○ Total Fat 9g
Saturated Fat 1g
Polyunsaturated Fat 2g
Monounsaturated Fat 5g

○ Cholesterol 61mg

○ Sodium 113mg

PREPARATION TIP
If halibut is unavailable, other firm fish, such as monkfish, shark, or cod, can be used.

Preparation Time: 40 minutes, plus 30 minutes marinating
Serves: 4

BAKED HALIBUT WITH APPLES

HALIBUT IS A LEAN, FIRM FISH WHICH, WHEN BAKED WITH APPLES AND
WHITE WINE, RETAINS ITS MOIST TEXTURE AND VALUABLE NUTRIENTS.
THIS LIGHT DISH MAY BE SERVED WITH NEW POTATOES AND
STEAMED BROCCOLI OR GREEN BEANS.

*juice and grated zest of 1 lemon, or juice of 2 limes
and grated zest of 1 lime
4 halibut steaks, each about 175g (6oz)
1½ tbsp olive oil
2 dessert apples, such as Granny Smiths, cored
and sliced into 5mm (¼in) rings
2 onions, thinly sliced
1 large red pepper, cored, deseeded, and sliced into thin rings
1–2 red or green chillies, deseeded and thinly sliced (optional)
4 tbsp chopped fresh flat-leaf parsley or dill
salt and freshly ground black pepper, to taste
4 tbsp dry white wine*

1 Place the lemon juice and zest in a shallow dish, then add the fish, turning it in the juice to coat both sides. Cover, and refrigerate for 30 minutes.

2 Preheat the oven to 220°C/425°F/Gas 7. Brush a baking dish with a little of the oil. Arrange half the apples in the bottom of the dish, then top with half the onions and pepper.

3 Place the fish on top, reserving the marinade, and sprinkle with the chillies, if using, and half the parsley. Repeat with another layer of the onions and pepper, and finally the apples, then season.

4 Pour the reserved marinade, wine, and remaining oil over the apples. Bake for 15–20 minutes, basting the fish occasionally with some of the juices. Remove from the oven, and leave to cool a little. Scatter the rest of the parsley on top before serving.

Soused Herrings

LIKE OTHER OILY FISH, HERRINGS ARE RICH IN OMEGA-3 FATTY ACIDS,

WHICH LOWER THE RISK OF HEART DISEASE. THIS DISH IS BASED

ON A CLASSIC BRITISH RECIPE AND IS BEST SERVED SIMPLY

WITH A SALAD AND NEW POTATOES.

1 onion, thinly sliced
4 herrings, each about 225g (7½oz),
gutted, boned, and heads removed
4 tsp English mustard
4 tsp brown sugar
4 tbsp chopped fresh parsley
1 bay leaf
10 black peppercorns
4 cloves
1–2 small dried chillies (optional)
100ml (3½fl oz) dry white wine
3 tbsp white wine vinegar
salt, to taste

1 Preheat the oven to 200°C/400°F/Gas 6. Place the onion in a small bowl, and cover with boiling water. Leave to stand for 1 minute, then drain. Refresh the onion in cold water, then drain well and set aside.

2 Dry the herrings with kitchen towels, and open them out on a board, skin-side down. Spread the mustard over the flesh, and sprinkle with the sugar. Divide the prepared onion between the herrings, and sprinkle with the parsley. Roll up the herrings, head-end first, to form thick rolls, and secure each one with a wooden skewer.

3 Arrange the fish rolls in a baking dish, then scatter over the herbs and spices. Pour the wine and vinegar over the fish, then season. Cover with foil, and bake for 25 minutes.

4 Increase the heat to 230°C/450°F/Gas 8. Remove the foil and bake, basting the fish frequently with the juices, for a further 10–15 minutes, until the herrings are tender and the juices have reduced. Leave to stand for about 10 minutes before serving.

★ STAR INGREDIENT

Herrings contain omega-3 fatty acids, which may help to lower cholesterol levels in the body. Along with reducing the risk of heart attacks, these beneficial oils may lower blood pressure.

EACH SERVING PROVIDES:

○ Calories 270

○ Protein 21g

○ Carbohydrate 8g
　 Fibre 1g

○ Total Fat 15g
　 Saturated Fat 4g
　 Polyunsaturated Fat 3g
　 Monounsaturated Fat 7g

○ Cholesterol 55mg

○ Sodium 139mg

SERVING TIP

This dish is delicious cold and can be made the day before it is served. Store, covered, in the refrigerator and remove an hour before serving.

Preparation Time: 60 minutes, plus 10 minutes standing
Serves: 4

GRILLED MACKEREL WITH CITRUS SALSA

MACKEREL PLAYS AN IMPORTANT PART IN THE HEALTHY HEART

KITCHEN AS IT CONTAINS VALUABLE OMEGA-3 FATTY ACIDS, WHICH

HELP TO LOWER CHOLESTEROL LEVELS. SERVE THIS DISH WITH

A COMBINATION OF WILD AND WHITE RICE.

4 mackerel fillets, each about 100g (3½oz)
juice of 1 lemon, and 1 tsp grated zest
2 tsp paprika (optional)
fresh mint leaves, to garnish

FOR THE SALSA
2 oranges, segmented and cut into 1cm (½in) pieces
2 large lemons, segmented and cut into 1cm (½in) pieces
½–1 tsp dried chilli flakes
1 tbsp chopped fresh mint or parsley
salt and freshly ground black pepper, to taste

1 Mix together the salsa ingredients in a bowl. Cover, and refrigerate for at least an hour to allow the flavours to develop.

2 Place the fish in a shallow dish, and spoon over the lemon juice and zest, rubbing them into the flesh. Cover, and refrigerate for 30 minutes.

3 Heat the grill to high. Sprinkle the paprika, if using, over each fillet, and grill the fish for 3–4 minutes on each side, until tender. Serve with the citrus salsa, and garnish with the mint leaves.

VARIATION
Baked Mackerel The mackerel can be baked in the oven instead of being grilled. Preheat the oven to 220°C/425°F/Gas 7. Follow steps 1 and 2, above, then place the fish fillets in a lightly oiled baking dish and sprinkle the paprika over each fillet. Spoon the citrus salsa over the fillets. Bake in the preheated oven for 10–15 minutes, until the fish is tender. Serve, garnished with the mint leaves.

✳ STAR INGREDIENT
Oranges are one of the best-known sources of vitamin C, which may help to prevent cell damage and consequently reduce the risk of heart disease.

EACH SERVING PROVIDES:

- Calories 270
- Protein 21g
- Carbohydrate 10g
  Fibre 1g
- Total Fat 17g
  Saturated Fat 4g
  Polyunsaturated Fat 4g
  Monounsaturated Fat 8g
- Cholesterol 54mg
- Sodium 86mg

PREPARATION TIP
The paprika adds a piquancy to the mackerel fillets but can be omitted if preferred.

Preparation Time: 30 minutes, plus 1 hour marinating
Serves: 4

GRILLED SARDINES WITH CHILLI TOMATO SALSA

FRESH SARDINES ARE PACKED WITH FLAVOUR AND FULL OF HEALTHY OMEGA-3 FATTY ACIDS, WHICH HELP TO LOWER BLOOD-CHOLESTEROL LEVELS, REDUCING THE RISK OF HEART DISEASE. THE PIQUANT CHILLI TOMATO SALSA ADDS A REFRESHING TANG.

4 sardines, each about 175g (6oz), gutted and boned
juice and grated zest of 1 lemon

FOR THE SALSA
4 plum tomatoes, skinned, deseeded, and finely chopped
1 small red or white onion, finely chopped
1–2 cloves garlic, crushed
1–2 green chillies, deseeded and finely chopped
small bunch of fresh flat-leaf parsley, dill, or mint, chopped
juice of 1 lemon and ½ tsp grated zest
salt and freshly ground black pepper, to taste

1 Cut three deep slashes down the sides of each sardine. Place the fish in a shallow dish, and sprinkle with the lemon juice and zest, rubbing them into the skin and flesh. Cover, and refrigerate for 30 minutes.

2 Mix together the salsa ingredients in a bowl. Cover, and refrigerate for 30 minutes to allow the flavours to develop.

3 Heat the grill to high. Grill the sardines for 3–4 minutes on each side, until tender and browned. Serve with the salsa.

VARIATION
Marinated Sardines Mix together 1 tablespoon reduced salt soy sauce, juice of 1 lime or lemon, plus 1 teaspoon grated zest, 1 stick of lemongrass, peeled and finely chopped, 3 spring onions, finely shredded, and 5 tablespoons rice wine or dry sherry. Follow step 3, above, then pour the marinade over the hot, grilled sardines. Leave to cool and serve with the salsa.

✱ STAR INGREDIENT
Like other citrus fruits, lemons are rich in vitamin C and potassium, which regulates blood pressure. Lemon pectin, found mainly in the skin around each segment, is reputed to help reduce blood-cholesterol levels.

EACH SERVING PROVIDES:

○ Calories 225

○ Protein 28g

○ Carbohydrate 3g
  Fibre 1g

○ Total Fat 11g
  Saturated Fat 3g
  Polyunsaturated Fat 4g
  Monounsaturated Fat 3g

○ Cholesterol 105mg

○ Sodium 156mg

SERVING TIP
This dish is best served simply with slices of good-quality wholemeal or seeded bread.

Preparation Time: 20 minutes, plus 30 minutes marinating
Serves: 4

GRILLED FISH CAKES WITH CUCUMBER SALSA

THESE DELICIOUS, LIGHTLY SPICED FISH CAKES ARE A NUTRITIOUS COMBINATION OF WHITE AND OILY FISH. SERVE THEM WITH NEW POTATOES, RICE, OR PASTA FOR A SATISFYING MAIN COURSE.

150g (5oz) mackerel fillets, skinned and cut into pieces
200g (7oz) hake fillets, skinned and cut into pieces
4 spring onions, finely chopped
1 red chilli, deseeded and finely chopped
1 clove garlic, crushed
100g (3½oz) cooked rice or barley
4 tbsp matzo meal or breadcrumbs
1 egg white
1 tsp finely grated lemon zest
salt and freshly ground black pepper, to taste
1 tbsp olive oil

FOR THE SALSA
1 cucumber, deseeded and finely chopped
1 clove garlic, crushed
1–2 chillies, deseeded and finely chopped
1 stick of lemongrass, peeled and finely chopped
juice of 2 lemons, plus ½ tsp grated zest
2 tbsp chopped fresh coriander

1 Mix together the ingredients for the salsa in a bowl. Cover, and refrigerate for 30 minutes to allow the flavours to develop.

2 Place the fish in a food processor, and process until finely chopped but not puréed. Mix with the remaining ingredients, except the oil, in a bowl. Cover, and refrigerate for 30 minutes. Divide the mixture into 8 portions and, using your hands, shape each portion into a flat cake.

3 Heat the grill to high. Brush the cakes with the oil, and grill for about 5 minutes on each side, until golden. (Alternatively, griddle the cakes for the same length of time.) Serve with the salsa.

✷ STAR INGREDIENT

Hake is an excellent source of low-fat protein. Both white and oily fish should be a regular part of a healthy diet.

EACH SERVING PROVIDES:

○ Calories 250

○ Protein 20g

○ Carbohydrate 19g
  Fibre 1g

○ Total Fat 12g
  Saturated Fat 2g
  Polyunsaturated Fat 3g
  Monounsaturated Fat 6g

○ Cholesterol 32mg

○ Sodium 96mg

PREPARATION TIPS

Other types of fish can be used but it is important to select two varieties: an oily fish, such as tuna or salmon; and a lean white fish, such as bream, halibut, or cod. If you have a mincer, use this instead of a food processor.

Preparation Time: 25 minutes, plus 30 minutes chilling
Serves: 4

Sea bass is naturally low in fat and high in iodine, protein, and selenium. It also contains useful amounts of vitamin E.

EACH SERVING PROVIDES:

○ Calories 235

○ Protein 36g

○ Carbohydrate 3g
   Fibre 2g

○ Total Fat 9g
   Saturated Fat 1g
   Polyunsaturated Fat 4g
   Monounsaturated Fat 3g

○ Cholesterol 140mg

○ Sodium 236mg

PREPARATION TIP
To make the fish even more fragrant, add a small cinnamon stick, 2 star anise, and a finely chopped stick of lemongrass to the cooking water.

Preparation Time: 20 minutes
Serves: 4

CHINESE STEAMED SEA BASS

THIS IS A CLASSIC, CHINESE-INSPIRED DISH THAT MAKES A SIMPLE, YET ATTRACTIVE MAIN COURSE FOR A DINNER PARTY. FLAVOURED WITH GINGER, GARLIC, AND SPRING ONIONS, THE DISH IS EXCELLENT SERVED WITH NOODLES OR RICE.

4 sea bass fillets, each about 175g (6oz)
4 spring onions, sliced into fine strips
1 carrot, sliced into fine strips
2.5cm (1in) piece of fresh ginger, sliced into fine strips
1 mild red chilli, deseeded and sliced into fine strips
2 tsp reduced salt soy sauce
1 tbsp mirin
2 tsp sake or dry sherry
2 tbsp sesame seeds, roasted in a dry frying pan

1 Place the fish on a plate, in a steamer. Arrange the vegetables, ginger, and chilli on top of each fillet, then spoon over the soy sauce, mirin, and sake. Cover, and steam for 10 minutes, or until the fish is opaque, flaky, and tender.

2 Place the fish and vegetables, with their cooking juices, on a warmed plate. Scatter the sesame seeds over the fish before serving. (The seeds can also be scattered over the accompanying noodles or rice.)

VARIATION

Chinese Steamed Chicken Replace the sea bass with 4 skinless chicken breasts, each about 125g (4oz), sliced into strips, and the carrot with 1 red pepper, deseeded and sliced into strips. Place the chicken on a plate, in a steamer. Cover and steam for 10 minutes. Remove from the heat and arrange the vegetables on top of the chicken, then spoon over the soy sauce, mirin, and sake. Cover, and steam for 5–10 minutes, until the chicken and vegetables are tender. To serve the chicken, follow step 2, above.

MONKFISH CURRY WITH CORIANDER

MOST KINDS OF FIRM-FLESHED WHITE FISH ARE SUITABLE

FOR THIS CREAMY, KORMA-STYLE CURRY. SERVE IT WITH PLAIN

BASMATI RICE, BULGAR, OR NOODLES.

1 tsp ground fennel seeds
1 tsp ground coriander
juice and grated zest of 1 lime
500g (1lb) monkfish, cut into bite-sized cubes
1 large onion, coarsely chopped
4 cloves garlic, chopped
2.5cm (1in) piece of fresh ginger, peeled and chopped
1–2 green chillies, deseeded and coarsely chopped
1 tbsp sunflower oil
½ tsp fennel seeds
2.5cm (1in) piece of cinnamon stick
1 bay leaf
300ml (½ pint) fish or chicken stock (see pages 118–19),
or white wine
100ml (3½fl oz) fat-free yogurt
freshly ground black pepper, to taste
fresh coriander, to garnish

★ STAR INGREDIENT

Spices may aid digestion and help to regulate the metabolism. Fennel seeds are reputed to be antispasmodic and diuretic.

EACH SERVING PROVIDES:

○ Calories 150

○ Protein 25g

○ Carbohydrate 4g
  Fibre 1g

○ Total Fat 5g
  Saturated Fat 1g
  Polyunsaturated Fat 3g
  Monounsaturated Fat 1g

○ Cholesterol 18mg

○ Sodium 77mg

PREPARATION TIPS

Try experimenting with different types of fish: white fish, including cod or halibut, or oily fish, such as mackerel or salmon, are delicious alternatives to the monkfish. Remember to remove the cinnamon stick and bay leaf before serving the curry.

Preparation Time: 50 minutes
Serves: 4

1 Mix together the spices and the lime juice and zest in a dish. Add the fish, turning it in the mixture. Cover, and refrigerate for 30 minutes.

2 Place the onion, garlic, ginger, and chillies in a food processor, then process into a smooth paste. Heat the oil in a saucepan. Add the fennel seeds, cinnamon stick, and bay leaf, and cook for 1 minute over a medium heat. Add the spice paste to the pan, and cook, stirring, for about 5 minutes, or until the mixture starts to colour.

3 Add the stock and cook, stirring frequently, for about 20 minutes, or until the mixture has thickened.

4 Add the fish with its marinade, then reduce the heat, and simmer for 10 minutes, or until the fish is tender. Stir in the yogurt and seasoning, then heat through. Garnish with the coriander before serving.

Tea-smoked Salmon

HOT-SMOKING IS A SIMPLE, TOTALLY FAT-FREE METHOD OF COOKING

THAT DOES NOT REQUIRE ANY SPECIALIST EQUIPMENT AND

SUITS MOST TYPES OF FISH. THIS FRAGRANT DISH CAN BE SERVED

WITH NEW POTATOES AND A SALAD.

4 salmon steaks, each about 125g (4oz)
juice of ½ lemon, ¼ tsp grated zest, and 2 strips
of lemon zest
freshly ground black pepper, to taste
2 tbsp black tea leaves
4–5 star anise, crushed
1–2 cinnamon sticks, crushed
a few sprigs of fresh thyme and rosemary

1 Sprinkle the fish with the lemon juice and zest. Cover, and refrigerate for about 1 hour.

2 Line an old, large, lidded wok or saucepan with a layer of heavy-duty foil, and place the pepper, tea leaves, star anise, cinnamon, thyme, and rosemary on top. Place a wire rack inside the wok or saucepan, then arrange the fish on top. Cover tightly with the lid.

3 Place the pan over a high heat until it starts smoking. Reduce the heat to low, and smoke for 10–15 minutes, until the fish is tender. Turn off the heat and leave to cool, with the lid on, for about 5 minutes.

VARIATION

Tea-smoked Chicken Marinate 4 skinless, boneless chicken breasts, each about 125g (4oz) in the lemon juice as in step 1, above, then steam the chicken for 10 minutes, until tender. Prepare the saucepan or wok as in step 2, above, substituting the chicken for the fish. Cover tightly. Follow step 3, above, cooking the chicken for 20–25 minutes, until tender and smoky.

✶ STAR INGREDIENT
Salmon is an oily fish that is rich in unsaturated fats, particularly omega-3 fatty acids, which may reduce the risk of heart disease.

EACH SERVING PROVIDES:

○ Calories 230

○ Protein 25g

○ Carbohydrate <1g
Fibre 0g

○ Total Fat 14g
Saturated Fat 2g
Polyunsaturated Fat 5g
Monounsaturated Fat 6g

○ Cholesterol 63mg

○ Sodium 56mg

PREPARATION TIP
Although any type of tea can be used, Lapsang Souchong is preferable, since it has a wonderfully smoky flavour.

Preparation Time: 25 minutes
Serves: 4

Chicken is a good source of low-fat protein as long as the skin is removed before cooking.

EACH SERVING PROVIDES:

○ Calories 245

○ Protein 28g

○ Carbohydrate 14g
Fibre 1g

○ Total Fat 10g
Saturated Fat 2g
Polyunsaturated Fat 4g
Monounsaturated Fat 4g

○ Cholesterol 96mg

○ Sodium 119mg

PREPARATION TIP

If the sauce is too watery at the end of the cooking time, increase the heat and boil rapidly, stirring frequently, until it has thickened.

Preparation Time: 1 hour, 25 minutes
Serves: 4

CHICKEN & PINEAPPLE CURRY

ALTHOUGH THIS RECIPE IS MADE WITH PINEAPPLE, PAPAYA IS
A SUITABLE ALTERNATIVE, SINCE BOTH FRUITS CONTAIN AN ENZYME
THAT TENDERIZES MEAT, MAKING IT EASIER TO DIGEST. SERVE THIS
FRAGRANT CURRY WITH PLAIN, STEAMED RICE.

1 onion, chopped
3 cloves garlic
2.5cm (1in) piece of fresh ginger, chopped
1 ripe pineapple, peeled, cored, and coarsely chopped
2–3 red chillies, deseeded and chopped
2 tsp coriander seeds, ground
2 cardamom pods, ground
½ tsp ground cinnamon
1 tbsp soft brown sugar
1 tbsp sunflower or light olive oil, plus extra for greasing
375ml (13fl oz) water
6 skinless, boneless chicken thighs, each about 75g (3oz)
6 tbsp fat-free yogurt
3–4 tbsp fresh coriander or dill, to garnish

1 Preheat the oven to 230°C/450°F/Gas 8. Arrange the onion, garlic, ginger, pineapple, and chillies in a baking dish. Spoon the spices, sugar, oil, and 4 tablespoons of the water over the onion mixture. Bake for 25 minutes, turning the mixture occasionally, until it starts to caramelize.

2 Heat a lightly oiled griddle and cook the chicken for 3–4 minutes on each side, until golden, then set aside and keep hot.

3 Transfer the pineapple mixture to a food processor, and blend into a smooth purée. Mix together the remaining water and the yogurt, then put them in a saucepan with the pineapple mixture.

4 Bring the mixture to a boil, then reduce the heat. Add the chicken and simmer, uncovered, for about 45 minutes, or until the sauce has reduced and thickened and the chicken is tender. Garnish with the coriander before serving.

TANDOORI CHICKEN

TENDER PIECES OF CHICKEN ARE MARINATED IN A COMBINATION
OF YOGURT AND SPICES IN THIS TRADITIONAL INDIAN
CELEBRATION DISH. IT MAKES A WONDERFUL, LIGHT MEAL THAT
MAY BE ACCOMPANIED BY RICE AND A SALAD.

★ STAR INGREDIENT

Ginger is a warming, aromatic spice with numerous health benefits. It may effectively relieve indigestion, stimulate the circulation, and combat colds and coughs.

EACH SERVING PROVIDES:

○ Calories 245

○ Protein 41g

○ Carbohydrate 5g
  Fibre <1g

○ Total Fat 9g
  Saturated Fat 2g
  Polyunsaturated Fat 2g
  Monounsaturated Fat 4g

○ Cholesterol 128mg

○ Sodium 188 mg

SERVING TIP

A good lunchtime main course, this dish may also be served cold as part of a buffet.

Preparation Time: 1 hour, 10 minutes, plus 8–12 hours marinating
Serves: 4

6 cloves garlic, chopped
5cm (2in) piece of fresh ginger, chopped
250ml (8fl oz) fat-free yogurt
juice of 2 limes and grated zest of 1 lime
2 tbsp ground coriander
1 tbsp sweet paprika
1 tbsp ground cumin
1 tbsp turmeric
1–2 tsp chilli powder
1 tsp ground cardamom
8 skinless chicken thighs, each about 75g (3oz)
quartered limes, to garnish

1 Place the garlic and ginger in a spice mill or food processor, and blend into a smooth paste. Add the yogurt, lime juice and zest, and the rest of the spices, and blend well.

2 Prick the chicken all over with a fork. Put the chicken in a baking dish, then spoon over two-thirds of the spice paste, rubbing it well into the meat. (Reserve the rest of the spice paste.) Leave to marinate, covered, for about 8–12 hours in the refrigerator.

3 Preheat the oven to 200°C/400°F/Gas 6. Line a baking sheet with foil. Put the marinated chicken on a rack placed over the lined baking sheet. Spread the reserved spice paste over the chicken, and bake for 45–60 minutes, until the chicken is tender. Serve with the lime quarters.

ORIENTAL GINGER CHICKEN

THE AROMATIC GARLIC, GINGER, AND SESAME OIL MARINADE ADDS

A CHINESE FLAVOUR TO THIS SIMPLE MAIN COURSE DISH.

SERVE IT WITH PLAIN RICE OR NOODLES AND

A MIXED LEAF SALAD.

*4 skinless, boneless chicken breasts, each about 125g (4oz),
sliced into 1cm (½in) strips*
*4 spring onions, finely shredded, green parts
removed and reserved*
1 carrot, sliced into fine strips
*100g (3½oz) shiitake mushrooms, stems discarded,
and caps thinly sliced*
100g (3½oz) thin asparagus tips or mangetout
freshly ground black pepper, to taste

FOR THE MARINADE
1–2 hot chillies, deseeded and finely chopped
1 clove garlic, finely chopped
2.5cm (1in) piece of fresh ginger, grated
1 tbsp reduced salt soy sauce
1 tbsp soft dark brown sugar or honey
1 tbsp toasted sesame oil

1 Combine the marinade ingredients. Place the chicken in a shallow dish, then add the marinade. Turn the chicken in the marinade, massaging it into the meat. Cover, and refrigerate for 30 minutes.

2 Place the chicken on a plate in a steamer. Spoon the marinade over the chicken. Arrange the vegetables, except the asparagus, over the chicken, and steam for 15–20 minutes, until the meat is tender.

3 Add the asparagus 5 minutes before the end of the cooking time, and cook, until just tender. Season, and garnish the chicken and vegetables with the reserved green parts of the spring onions.

✷ STAR INGREDIENT
Asparagus is a rich source of folate, which is thought to help protect against heart disease.

EACH SERVING PROVIDES:

○ Calories 230

○ Protein 29g

○ Carbohydrate 7g
   Fibre 1g

○ Total Fat 10g
   Saturated Fat 2g
   Polyunsaturated Fat 3g
   Monounsaturated Fat 4g

○ Cholesterol 106mg

○ Sodium 292mg

PREPARATION TIP
Try using guinea fowl instead of chicken. It has a pleasant, mild, gamey flavour.

Preparation Time: 50 minutes, plus 30 minutes marinating
Serves: 4

CHICKEN FRIKADELES

THESE HERBY CHICKEN MEATBALLS ARE BAKED IN A RICH,

SPICY TOMATO SAUCE. THE MEATBALLS CAN BE SERVED ON A BED

OF STEAMED BROWN RICE OR PASTA WITH A STEAMED, GREEN

LEAFY VEGETABLE OR GREEN SALAD.

1 small onion, chopped
3 celery sticks, with their green leaves, chopped
1 small hot chilli, deseeded and chopped
small bunch of fresh parsley, stalks removed
1–2 sprigs of thyme, leaves finely chopped
350g (11½oz) minced chicken or turkey
75g (2½oz) cooked pearl barley
1 egg white
3–4 tbsp dried breadcrumbs or matzo meal
salt and freshly ground black pepper, to taste
1 quantity Spicy Tomato Sauce (see page 120)

1 Place the onion, celery, chilli, and parsley in a food processor, and process until finely chopped but not puréed.

2 Transfer the mixture to a bowl, then add the thyme, chicken, barley, egg white, breadcrumbs, and seasoning, and mix well. Cover, and refrigerate for about 1 hour.

3 Preheat the oven to 200°C/400°F/Gas 6. Cover the bottom of a baking dish with half the tomato sauce, then place rounded tablespoonfuls of the chicken mixture on top. Cover with the remaining sauce, and bake, uncovered, basting the chicken balls occasionally, for 30–45 minutes, until they are cooked and tender.

✱ STAR INGREDIENT
Celery contains fibre and a range of vitamins and minerals that all contribute to good health.

EACH SERVING PROVIDES:

○ Calories 240

○ Protein 24g

○ Carbohydrate 25g
Fibre 4g

○ Total Fat 6g
Saturated Fat 2g
Polyunsaturated Fat 2g
Monounsaturated Fat 2g

○ Cholesterol 74mg

○ Sodium 160mg

PREPARATION TIP
This dish improves if kept overnight in the refrigerator. Store covered, removing from the refrigerator an hour before serving.

Preparation Time: 55 minutes, plus 1 hour chilling
Serves: 4

CHICKEN CASSOULET

THIS SATISFYING, SUBSTANTIAL DISH IS PERFECT "COMFORT FOOD"

FOR A COLD WINTER'S EVENING. THE NUTRITIOUS COMBINATION

OF HIGH-FIBRE BEANS, GARLIC, VEGETABLES, AND CHICKEN

MAKES A COMPLETE MEAL IN ITSELF.

1½ tbsp olive oil
6 skinless, boneless chicken thighs, each about 75g (3oz),
cut into bite-sized pieces
1 large onion, finely chopped
4 cloves garlic, coarsely chopped
1 large carrot, coarsely chopped
5 tbsp water
150g (5oz) brown cap or flat mushrooms, sliced
15g (½oz) dried ceps, rehydrated in hot water for 20 minutes (optional)
3 tbsp chopped fresh thyme, or ¾ tsp dried thyme
200g (7oz) dried flageolet or haricot beans, cooked, or
400g (13oz) canned beans in water
300–400ml (10–14fl oz) hot chicken or vegetable stock
(see pages 118–19)
salt and freshly ground black pepper, to taste

1 Preheat the oven to 200°C/400°F/Gas 6. Heat the oil in a large, heavy-based saucepan. Add the chicken pieces and cook over a medium heat for 3–4 minutes, until browned all over, then set aside. Add the onion, garlic, and carrot to the pan, and cook for a further 1–2 minutes.

2 Add the water to the pan, and cook the vegetables over a medium heat for 5–6 minutes, stirring occasionally, until the water evaporates and the onion starts to brown. Remove the pan from the heat, then stir in the browned chicken and all the mushrooms.

3 Spoon a layer of the chicken and vegetables into an ovenproof casserole. Sprinkle with a third of the thyme and a third of the beans. Continue to layer until all the ingredients have been used.

4 Pour the stock over the layered ingredients and season. Cover, and bake for 45 minutes, stirring occasionally. Uncover, and bake for a further 10–15 minutes, until the chicken is tender.

✴ STAR INGREDIENT
Flageolet beans, like other beans, are a good source of soluble fibre, which may lower blood-cholesterol levels and thus reduce the risk of heart disease.

EACH SERVING PROVIDES:

○ Calories 346

○ Protein 33g

○ Carbohydrate 32g
Fibre 10g

○ Total Fat 10g
Saturated Fat 2g
Polyunsaturated Fat 2g
Monounsaturated Fat 6g

○ Cholesterol 64mg

○ Sodium 211mg

PREPARATION TIP
Add extra stock or water to the cassoulet in step 4 if it appears too dry.

Preparation Time: 1 hour, 20 minutes
Serves: 4

CHICKEN NOODLE STIR-FRY

STIR-FRYING IS A CLASSIC LOW-FAT METHOD OF COOKING, AND
IS INCREDIBLY VERSATILE. THIS SIMPLE DISH INCLUDES A HEALTHY
COMBINATION OF GARLIC, CHILLIES, SHIITAKE MUSHROOMS, AND
BROCCOLI, WHICH ARE KNOWN TO BE GOOD FOR THE HEART.

★ STAR INGREDIENT

Broccoli is rich in many vitamins
and minerals, particularly the
antioxidants vitamin C and beta-
carotene, as well as folate,
which are all thought to protect
against heart disease.

EACH SERVING PROVIDES:

○ Calories 460

○ Protein 38g

○ Carbohydrate 54g
  Fibre 1g

○ Total Fat 10g
  Saturated Fat 2g
  Polyunsaturated Fat 4g
  Monounsaturated Fat 3g

○ Cholesterol 88mg

○ Sodium 379mg

PREPARATION TIP

Skinless chicken breast is low in
fat and consequently can dry
out during cooking. To retain
a moist texture, cook it quickly
until tender.

Preparation Time: 40 minutes
Serves: 4

1 tbsp sunflower or light olive oil
½ tbsp toasted sesame oil
4 skinless, boneless chicken breasts, each about 125g (4oz),
sliced into 1cm (½in) strips
5 tbsp water
4–5 cloves garlic, thinly sliced
2–3 mild red chillies, deseeded and cut into fine strips
1 bunch spring onions, chopped, the green parts reserved, to garnish
150g (5oz) shiitake mushrooms, stems discarded,
and caps thickly sliced
1 tbsp reduced salt soy sauce
300ml (½ pint) chicken stock (see page 119)
1 tsp cornflour, mixed with 1 tbsp white wine
150g (5oz) broccoli florets, lightly steamed
250g (8oz) dried thin rice noodles, soaked
in boiling water for 3 minutes

① Heat the sunflower and sesame oils in a large wok or frying pan.
Add the chicken, and stir-fry over a high heat for 4–5 minutes, until the
meat has browned. Remove the meat from the wok and keep warm.

② Reduce the heat to medium. Add the water and mix it with the wok
juices. Add the garlic, chillies, and spring onions, reserving the green
parts. Stir-fry for a further 3–4 minutes, until the onions start to soften.

③ Add the shiitake mushrooms and the soy sauce, and stir-fry for
2–3 minutes, until they have softened. Add the stock and bring the
mixture to a boil. Reduce the heat, then simmer gently for 15 minutes,
or until the stock has slightly reduced.

④ Increase the heat, stir in the cornflour mixture, and bring to a boil.
Add the chicken, broccoli, and noodles. Cook for 5–6 minutes, until all
the ingredients are heated through and the chicken is tender. Garnish
with the green parts of the spring onions before serving.

VENISON STEAKS WITH THREE-PEPPER SALSA

LEANER AND CONSEQUENTLY LOWER IN FAT THAN MOST OTHER RED MEATS, VENISON IS NOW READILY AVAILABLE IN SHOPS. FOR THIS RECIPE, OTHER LEAN MEAT STEAKS CAN ALTERNATIVELY BE USED, IF DESIRED.

★ STAR INGREDIENT
Due to its high essential oil content, fresh rosemary is thought to benefit the entire nervous system.

EACH SERVING PROVIDES:

○ Calories 300

○ Protein 41g

○ Carbohydrate 9g
Fibre 3g

○ Total Fat 11g
Saturated Fat 2g
Polyunsaturated Fat 4g
Monounsaturated Fat 5g

○ Cholesterol 88mg

○ Sodium 103mg

SERVING TIP
Serve the venison with a baked potato and a green salad or steamed vegetables.

Preparation Time: 35 minutes, plus 1 hour chilling
Serves: 4

1 tbsp olive oil
2 cloves garlic, crushed
juice of ½ lemon
1 tbsp English mustard
1 tbsp chopped fresh rosemary
4 venison steaks, each about 125g (4oz)

FOR THE SALSA
1 large red pepper, halved, cored, and deseeded
1 large yellow or orange pepper, halved, cored, and deseeded
1 large green pepper, halved, cored, and deseeded
1 tbsp sunflower oil
1 small red onion, finely chopped
1 clove garlic, crushed
1–2 chillies, deseeded and finely chopped (optional)
2 tbsp wine vinegar
2 tbsp chopped fresh thyme
salt and freshly ground black pepper, to taste

1 Mix together the oil, garlic, lemon juice, mustard, and rosemary to form a thick paste. Spread the paste evenly over both sides of each steak. Cover, and refrigerate for about 1 hour.

2 Heat the grill to high. Lightly brush the peppers with the oil, and grill for 5–7 minutes, until charred and blistered. Transfer the peppers to a plastic bag and seal. Leave for 5 minutes, then peel under cold, running water and chop finely.

3 Place the peppers and the rest of the salsa ingredients in a bowl. Cover, and refrigerate for 30 minutes. Heat the grill to high. Grill the steaks for 5–6 minutes on each side, or until cooked according to preference. Serve with the salsa.

★ STAR INGREDIENT
Bulgar wheat is low in sodium and high in carbohydrates, making it a useful staple in a healthy heart diet.

EACH SERVING PROVIDES:

○ Calories 190

○ Protein 22g

○ Carbohydrate 14g
  Fibre 2g

○ Total Fat 6g
  Saturated Fat 1g
  Polyunsaturated Fat 3g
  Monounsaturated Fat 1g

○ Cholesterol 44mg

○ Sodium 83mg

PREPARATION TIP
Try adding different vegetables, such as Brussels sprouts, cabbage, or mushrooms to these burgers, or even fruits like apples and pears.

Preparation Time: 30 minutes, plus 1 hour chilling
Serves: 4

VENISON BURGERS

THESE JUICY BURGERS WILL SATISFY THE CRAVINGS OF ANY CARNIVORE. I SOMETIMES INCLUDE A CLOVE OF MASHED GARLIC IN THE BURGER MIXTURE, WHICH GIVES IT A WONDERFUL TASTE AND AROMA. SERVE THE BURGERS IN A BUN, OR WITH A BAKED POTATO AND SALAD.

350g (11½oz) minced venison
1 onion, finely chopped or minced
2 celery sticks, finely chopped or minced
1 small carrot, finely grated or minced
50g (1½oz) bulgar, soaked in hot water for 30 minutes, drained, and squeezed dry
4 tbsp chopped fresh flat-leaf parsley, stalks removed
1 egg white
salt and freshly ground black pepper, to taste
1 tbsp sunflower oil

TO GARNISH
2 shallots, thinly sliced
4 sprigs of redcurrants
lettuce leaves

1 .Place all the ingredients, except the oil and garnishes, in a large bowl, and knead well until thoroughly combined. (This can alternatively be done in a food processor with either the beater or the dough-hook attachment.) Cover, and refrigerate for about 1 hour.

2 Heat the grill to high. Divide the mixture into 4 equal portions, then shape each one into a burger about 2.5cm (1in) thick. Lightly brush each burger with the oil, then grill for 5–8 minutes on each side, until browned. (Alternatively, griddle the burgers for the same length of time.) Garnish with the shallots, sprigs of redcurrants, and lettuce leaves.

VARIATION
Chicken Burgers Replace the venison with 350g (11½oz) minced chicken or turkey. Increase the quantity of bulgar to 75g (3oz) and flavour the mixture with 2 sticks of lemongrass, peeled and finely chopped, and 1–2 red chillies, deseeded and finely chopped. Replace the parsley with 4 tablespoons of chopped fresh coriander.

RABBIT RAGOUT

RABBIT IS A MUCH-NEGLECTED MEAT, BUT IT HAS THE ADVANTAGE OF

BEING VERY LOW IN FAT AND CHOLESTEROL. SERVE THIS

RICH STEW WITH RICE OR PASTA, OR WITH CHUNKS OF WHOLEMEAL

BREAD TO MOP UP THE JUICES.

★ STAR INGREDIENT
Shallots contain sulphur compounds that may help to control cholesterol levels, as well as quercetin, which may protect against heart disease.

EACH SERVING PROVIDES:

○ Calories 280

○ Protein 32g

○ Carbohydrate 16g
Fibre 2g

○ Total Fat 10g
Saturated Fat 3g
Polyunsaturated Fat 3g
Monounsaturated Fat 4g

○ Cholesterol 66mg

○ Sodium 159mg

PREPARATION TIP
This recipe can alternatively be made with venison, chicken, or turkey.

Preparation Time: 1 hour, 15 minutes, plus 30 minutes marinating
Serves: 4

2 tbsp lemon juice
grated zest of ½ orange
1 tbsp olive oil
500g (1lb) boneless rabbit legs, cut into bite-sized pieces
6 small shallots, quartered
6 large cloves garlic, quartered
3 celery sticks, finely chopped
juice of 2 oranges
300ml (½ pint) chicken or vegetable stock (see pages 118–19)
bouquet garni, made up of 3 sprigs of thyme,
2 sprigs of rosemary, and 1 bay leaf
salt and freshly ground black pepper, to taste
100g (3½oz) ready-to-eat dried prunes
fresh thyme, to garnish

1 Combine the lemon juice, orange zest, and half the oil, then pour the mixture over the rabbit in a shallow dish. Turn the meat in the marinade. Cover, and refrigerate for 30 minutes.

2 Heat a heavy-based saucepan over a medium heat, and fry the rabbit for 8 minutes, turning occasionally, until browned. Set aside, and keep warm. Heat the remaining oil in the pan. Add the shallots, garlic, and celery, and fry for 5 minutes, or until browned. Add the orange juice, stock, bouquet garni, and seasoning. Bring to a boil, then reduce the heat and simmer for 2 minutes. Add the rabbit, and bring to a rapid boil, turning the rabbit pieces in the boiling liquid, then season.

3 Reduce the heat and add the prunes. Cover, and simmer, skimming away any froth, for 45 minutes, or until the rabbit is tender. Remove the rabbit, and keep hot. Remove and discard the bouquet garni, then return the liquid to the boil, and boil hard for 8–10 minutes, until the liquid has reduced by half. Return the rabbit to the pan and heat through. Garnish with the thyme before serving.

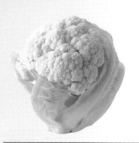

FRUITY VEGETABLE CURRY

THIS AROMATIC BLEND OF GARLIC, GINGER, CINNAMON, AND STOCK

MAKES A RICH SAUCE FOR BABY VEGETABLES AND SWEET DESSERT APPLES.

BASED ON A CLASSIC RECIPE, THIS CURRY IS BEST SERVED WITH RICE

AND TOPPED WITH A SPOONFUL OF LOW-FAT YOGURT.

✱ STAR INGREDIENT

Cauliflower is full of valuable nutrients, including potassium, fibre, vitamins C and E, folate, and beta-carotene, which together may help to protect against heart disease.

EACH SERVING PROVIDES:

- ○ Calories 130
- ○ Protein 5g
- ○ Carbohydrate 18g
  Fibre 4g
- ○ Total Fat 6g
  Saturated Fat 1g
  Polyunsaturated Fat 2g
  Monounsaturated Fat 3g
- ○ Cholesterol 0mg
- ○ Sodium 111mg

Preparation Time: 35 minutes
Serves: 4

1 onion, finely chopped
4 cloves garlic, chopped
2.5cm (1in) piece of fresh ginger, chopped
1 carrot, coarsely chopped
1 tbsp groundnut oil
2 red chillies, deseeded and chopped
1 tbsp mustard seeds
4 cardamom pods
1 small cinnamon stick
½ tsp turmeric
4 tbsp cider or white wine vinegar
2 dessert apples, peeled, cored, and coarsely chopped
400ml (14fl oz) vegetable stock (see page 118), or water
1 tbsp honey or brown sugar
salt and freshly ground black pepper, to taste
400g (13oz) baby vegetables, such as cauliflower,
broccoli, or cabbage, quartered and lightly steamed
2 tbsp fresh coriander, to garnish

1 In a food processor, blend together the onion, garlic, ginger, and carrot into a thick paste.

2 Heat the oil in a heavy-based saucepan. Add the chillies, mustard seeds, and spices. Fry over a medium heat until the mustard seeds start to pop and emit a pleasant, toasted aroma. Add the onion paste and cook over a high heat, stirring frequently, for 5–6 minutes, until the mixture starts to colour. If the mixture becomes too dry, add 3–4 tablespoons of water.

3 Add the vinegar, apples, stock, honey, and seasoning. Bring to a boil, then reduce the heat. Simmer, uncovered, for 10 minutes, or until the apples are tender. Add the vegetables and simmer for 4–5 minutes to heat through. Garnish with the coriander before serving.

Broad Bean & Artichoke Stew

THIS LIGHT, YET SATISFYING SUMMER STEW CONTAINS A HEALTHY COMBINATION OF HIGH-FIBRE BROAD BEANS AND VITAMIN-RICH VEGETABLES. SERVE IT WITH SUNFLOWER SEED BREAD OR RICE.

1 tbsp olive oil
1 bunch of spring onions, shredded
4–5 cloves garlic, coarsely chopped
2 large carrots, chopped
2 celery sticks, finely chopped
500ml (17fl oz) vegetable stock (see pages 118–19)
bouquet garni, made up of 2–3 sprigs of thyme,
1–2 sprigs of rosemary, and 2 strips of lemon zest
400g (13oz) canned artichoke hearts, drained and quartered
400g (13oz) broad beans or canned chickpeas in water
juice of 1 lemon, mixed with 1 tsp sugar
salt and freshly ground black pepper, to taste
sprigs of fresh thyme, to garnish

1 Heat the oil in a heavy-based saucepan. Add the spring onions, garlic, carrots, and celery. Sauté over a medium heat for 5–8 minutes, until the vegetables have softened. Add the stock and bouquet garni, then bring to a boil. Cook for 4–5 minutes, until the liquid has reduced.

2 Reduce the heat, then add the artichoke hearts and broad beans to the pan. Simmer, half-covered, for 30–45 minutes, until most of the liquid has evaporated. Stir in the lemon juice mixture. Season, and garnish with the thyme before serving.

VARIATION
This recipe can alternatively be made with chicken breast. Slice 4 skinless, boneless chicken breasts, each about 125g (4oz), into 1cm (1/2in) strips. Cook them on a dry skillet, non-stick frying pan, or griddle for 3–4 minutes on each side, until browned. Add the chicken to the stew 10 minutes before the end of the cooking time.

★ STAR INGREDIENT
Broad beans are a good source of beta-carotene and soluble fibre and also contain some iron and vitamins C and E.

EACH SERVING PROVIDES:

○ Calories 181

○ Protein 13g

○ Carbohydrate 24g
  Fibre 11g

○ Total Fat 5g
  Saturated Fat 1g
  Polyunsaturated Fat 1g
  Monounsaturated Fat 3g

○ Cholesterol 0mg

○ Sodium 145mg

PREPARATION TIP
Chicken stock can be used instead of the vegetable stock, if preferred.

Preparation Time: 1 hour, 10 minutes
Serves: 4

CHINESE MIXED MUSHROOM STEW

IN ASIA, EATING ORIENTAL MUSHROOMS IS RECOMMENDED FOR A LONG AND HEALTHY LIFE. THEY ARE USED IN ABUNDANCE IN THIS DISH, WHICH IS DELICIOUS SERVED WITH RICE, NOODLES, OR BULGAR.

2 tbsp peanut or sesame oil
100g (3½oz) shallots, quartered
4 cloves garlic, thickly sliced
1–2 mild chillies, deseeded and finely chopped (optional)
125g (4oz) oyster mushrooms, broken into chunks
100g (3½oz) shiitake mushrooms, or 50g (2oz) dried shiitake, rehydrated in hot water for 20 minutes, stems discarded, and caps sliced
1 tbsp reduced salt soy sauce
400ml (14fl oz) vegetable or chicken stock (see pages 118–19)
250g (8oz) dried thin rice noodles, soaked in boiling water for 3 minutes
2 tbsp chopped fresh dill, to garnish

1 Heat the oil in a wok or heavy-based frying pan. Add the shallots, garlic, and chillies, if using, and stir-fry over a high heat for 3–4 minutes, until they start to brown. Add the oyster and shiitake mushrooms and stir-fry for a further 4–5 minutes, until the mushrooms have softened. Add the soy sauce and stir-fry for 1–2 minutes.

2 Add the stock, and bring to a boil. Reduce the heat and simmer for 15 minutes, until the stock has reduced.

3 Increase the heat to medium, add the noodles and cook, folding the noodles into the mushroom sauce, until almost all of the liquid has evaporated and the noodles are glossy. Garnish with the dill, before serving.

✳ STAR INGREDIENT

Studies have found that oriental mushrooms, including shiitake and oyster, may help to lower blood-cholesterol levels, possibly even reducing the effects of saturated fat in the body.

EACH SERVING PROVIDES:

○ Calories 360

○ Protein 9g

○ Carbohydrate 60g
Fibre 1g

○ Total Fat 8g
Saturated Fat 2g
Polyunsaturated Fat 2g
Monounsaturated Fat 3g

○ Cholesterol 0mg

○ Sodium 285mg

PREPARATION TIP

Use portobello or brown cap mushrooms instead of oyster mushrooms, if desired.

Preparation Time: 40 minutes
Serves: 4

MIXED GRAIN CASSOULET

SERVE THIS WARMING AND SUBSTANTIAL WINTER DISH WITH

A CHUNK OF WHOLEMEAL BREAD TO MOP UP THE JUICES. A GLASS

OF FULL-BODIED RED WINE MAKES A FINE ACCOMPANIMENT.

★ STAR INGREDIENT
Tofu is low in fat and rich in potassium, calcium, and isoflavones, which may reduce the risk of heart disease.

EACH SERVING PROVIDES:

○ Calories 340

○ Protein 14g

○ Carbohydrate 52g
Fibre 7g

○ Total Fat 9g
Saturated Fat 1g
Polyunsaturated Fat 2g
Monounsaturated Fat 5g

○ Cholesterol 0mg

○ Sodium 309mg

PREPARATION TIPS
You can prepare the cassoulet in advance and store it, covered, in the refrigerator for up to 2 days. Wheat berries are whole wheat grains and are readily available from health food shops.

Preparation Time: 2 hours, 25 minutes, plus soaking overnight
Serves: 4

60g (2oz) wheat berries, soaked overnight
60g (2oz) millet, soaked overnight
60g (2oz) pearl barley, soaked overnight
1½ tbsp olive oil
1 large onion, coarsely chopped
3 carrots, coarsely chopped
2–3 celery sticks, coarsely chopped
50g (1½oz) dried shiitake mushrooms, rehydrated in
100ml (3½fl oz) boiling water for 30 minutes, stems discarded,
and caps thickly sliced, and the soaking water reserved
150g (5oz) smoked tofu, cubed
bouquet garni, made up of 3–4 sprigs of thyme,
1–2 sprigs of marjoram, and 2 strips of lemon zest
1 tsp caraway seeds
freshly ground black pepper, to taste
500ml (17fl oz) chicken or vegetable stock
(see pages 118–19)
1 tbsp reduced salt soy sauce

1 Preheat the oven to 200°C/400°F/Gas 6. Drain the wheat berries, millet, and pearl barley, and mix together. Heat the oil in a large frying pan, and add the onion, carrots, and celery. Sauté over a medium heat for 5–8 minutes, until the onion starts to brown. Stir in the mushrooms and cook for a further 3 minutes.

2 Arrange a third of the grains in the base of a large casserole, and top with a third of the vegetable mixture and half of the tofu. Cover with another layer of grains, vegetables, and the rest of the tofu. Top with a final layer of grains and vegetables.

3 Place the bouquet garni over the grains and vegetables. Scatter the caraway seeds over the top and season. Pour in the stock, soy sauce, and reserved mushroom water. Cover, and bake for 1½–2 hours, until the grains are tender. Check the casserole occasionally, adding extra water if it becomes too dry.

✳ STAR INGREDIENT
Chick-peas are a low-fat source of protein, and are rich in soluble fibre.

EACH SERVING PROVIDES:

○ Calories 195

○ Protein 7g

○ Carbohydrate 21g
Fibre 5g

○ Total Fat 10g
Saturated Fat 1g
Polyunsaturated Fat 2g
Monounsaturated Fat 6g

○ Cholesterol 0mg

○ Sodium 19mg

BUYING TIP
Canned beans are a convenient alternative to dried. Make sure you buy them in water, rather than in brine, or salt and sugar.

Preparation Time: 2¼ hours, plus 8 hours soaking
Serves: 4

ROASTED RED PEPPER & CHICK-PEA SALAD

SWEET RED PEPPERS COMPLEMENT THE NUTTY FLAVOUR OF THE CHICK-PEAS IN THIS SIMPLE, COLOURFUL SALAD. IT MAKES A DELICIOUS ACCOMPANIMENT TO GRILLED MEAT OR FISH.

100g (3½oz) dried chick-peas, soaked overnight
4 red peppers, cored, deseeded, and quartered

FOR THE DRESSING
1 tbsp balsamic vinegar
2 tbsp extra-virgin olive oil
4 spring onions, finely chopped
1 clove garlic, finely chopped
2 tbsp chopped mixed fresh herbs,
such as parsley, thyme, and sage
salt and freshly ground black pepper,
to taste

1 Place the soaked chick-peas in a large saucepan, and cover with plenty of water. Bring to a boil, then reduce the heat and simmer, half-covered, for 1½–2 hours, until the chick-peas are tender. Meanwhile, mix together the dressing ingredients in a large bowl.

2 Heat the grill to high. Brush the skins of the peppers with a little of the dressing, then grill for 8–10 minutes, until the skins have blistered and blackened. Place the peppers in a plastic bag and leave for 5 minutes, then peel and slice. Stir the peppers into the dressing, then add the chick-peas, and mix well. Leave to cool before serving.

SALADS *This collection of fresh, delicious, and mouthwatering salads can be served as starters, accompaniments, or light main meals. If you do not go overboard on oil-laden dressings, salads are impressively low-fat sources of vitamins, minerals, and fibre.*

ROASTED GARLIC & COURGETTE SALAD

GARLIC IS AN IMPORTANT INGREDIENT IN THE HEALTHY HEART

KITCHEN. IT LOSES ITS PUNGENCY WHEN ROASTED, BECOMING SOFT,

CREAMY, AND MELLOW-TASTING.

12–16 large cloves garlic, peeled and quartered
juice of 1 orange and 1 tsp grated zest
1 tbsp olive oil
2–3 cloves (optional)
1–2 tsp brown sugar
6 courgettes, sliced with a potato peeler into ribbons
salt and freshly ground black pepper, to taste
1 tbsp chopped fresh dill or lemon thyme

1 Preheat the oven to 200°C/400°F/Gas 6. Place the garlic in a baking dish, then spoon over 3 tablespoons of the orange juice and the zest, oil, cloves, if using, and sugar. Cover with foil, and bake for 15–20 minutes, until the garlic starts to soften.

2 Pour boiling water over the courgettes and blanch for a few seconds until slightly softened. Drain well and pat dry with a kitchen towel, getting rid of as much moisture as possible.

3 Increase the oven setting to 230°C/450°F/Gas 8. Uncover the baking dish, then stir in the courgettes, and the remaining orange juice. Bake for a further 10–15 minutes, until the garlic and courgettes start to caramelize. Season, and sprinkle with the fresh herbs. Serve either hot or at room temperature.

✷ STAR INGREDIENT

The benefits of garlic are wide-ranging – it has been shown to improve the circulation, as well as to reduce both blood pressure and blood-cholesterol levels.

EACH SERVING PROVIDES:

○ Calories 80

○ Protein 3g

○ Carbohydrate 7g
Fibre 2g

○ Total Fat 4g
Saturated Fat <1g
Polyunsaturated Fat <1g
Monounsaturated Fat 3g

○ Cholesterol 0mg

○ Sodium 3mg

SERVING TIP

When roasted, garlic makes a wonderfully creamy, low-fat sandwich spread.

Preparation Time: 45 minutes
Serves: 4

CARAMELIZED ONION & POTATO SALAD

THE CARAMELIZED ONIONS LEND A DELICIOUS SWEETNESS TO THE

WARM NEW POTATOES. AS AN ADDED BONUS, POTATOES PROVIDE

LONG-TERM ENERGY, AS WELL AS FIBRE AND VITAMIN C.

500g (1lb) small salad potatoes
2 large onions, thinly sliced
4 tbsp water
2 tbsp olive or sunflower oil
6 tbsp balsamic vinegar
salt and freshly ground black pepper,
to taste
1 tsp caraway seeds, roasted in a dry frying pan,
and crushed
4 tbsp chopped, fresh flat-leaf parsley or mint

1 Steam the potatoes for 15 minutes, or until tender, then keep hot.

2 Meanwhile, put the onions and water in a small saucepan and bring to a boil. Reduce the heat, cover, and simmer for 10 minutes, or until the onion is tender and the water has evaporated.

3 Add the oil to the saucepan, and cook, stirring constantly, for a further 5 minutes, or until the onions start to caramelize. Add the vinegar and bring to a boil. Cook for 1–2 minutes, until the liquid has reduced and is glossy.

4 Pour the onion mixture over the hot potatoes in a large bowl, and mix well. Cover the bowl with a tea towel and leave the potatoes to cool to room temperature. Season to taste, and sprinkle with the caraway seeds and flat-leaf parsley before serving.

✶ STAR INGREDIENT

Onions, like garlic, contain allicin compounds that may help to fight infections and lower blood-cholesterol levels, as well as to protect against cancer.

EACH SERVING PROVIDES:

○ Calories 190

○ Protein 4g

○ Carbohydrate 27g
    Fibre 3g

○ Total Fat 8g
    Saturated Fat 1g
    Polyunsaturated Fat 1g
    Monounsaturated Fat 6g

○ Cholesterol 0mg

○ Sodium 15mg

PREPARATION TIP

Do not peel the potatoes – wash and scrub them instead to retain their fibre and vitamin contents.

Preparation Time: 25 minutes, plus 5 minutes cooling
Serves: 4

✴ STAR INGREDIENT
Grapefruit contains useful amounts of pectin, which has been found to lower levels of cholesterol in the blood.

EACH SERVING PROVIDES:

○ Calories 120

○ Protein 3g

○ Carbohydrate 17g
  Fibre 7g

○ Total Fat 4g
  Saturated Fat <1g
  Polyunsaturated Fat <1g
  Monounsaturated Fat 3g

○ Cholesterol 0mg

○ Sodium 28mg

Preparation Time: 15 minutes
Serves: 4

FENNEL & RUBY GRAPEFRUIT SALAD

THIS REFRESHING SALAD IS EXCELLENT WITH GRILLED FISH OR CHICKEN. LIKE OTHER CITRUS FRUITS, GRAPEFRUIT CONTAINS USEFUL AMOUNTS OF VITAMIN C, WHILE FENNEL IS A WELL-KNOWN DIURETIC.

2 large fennel bulbs, cored and thinly sliced,
fronds reserved, to garnish
2 large ruby grapefruit, segmented
1 small red or white onion, thinly sliced into rings
1 red chilli, deseeded and finely chopped
1 tbsp hazelnut oil
2 tsp clear honey
2 tbsp chopped fresh dill
salt and freshly ground black pepper, to taste

Combine the fennel (reserving the fronds to garnish) and grapefruit in a large serving bowl. Add the rest of the ingredients, then mix well until combined. Garnish with the reserved fennel fronds.

VARIATION
Orange and Chicory Salad Replace the fennel and grapefruit with 3 oranges, segmented, and 3 heads of chicory, thinly sliced.

BEETROOT SALAD WITH HONEY & YOGURT DRESSING

BEETROOT IS ONE OF NATURE'S MOST EFFECTIVE DETOXIFIERS, HELPING TO CLEANSE BOTH THE LIVER AND THE KIDNEYS. ITS NATURAL SWEETNESS ENHANCES THE FLAVOUR OF THE PINEAPPLE.

300g (10oz) raw beetroot, coarsely grated
1 small pineapple, peeled, cored, and chopped
3 shallots or 1 small onion, finely chopped

FOR THE DRESSING
juice of 1 lemon
2 tbsp honey mustard
3 tbsp fat-free Greek yogurt
1 tbsp olive or sunflower oil
salt and freshly ground black pepper, to taste

Mix together the dressing ingredients, and pour over the beetroot, pineapple, and shallots. Refrigerate for about 1 hour before serving.

EACH SERVING PROVIDES:

○ Calories 110

○ Protein 2g

○ Carbohydrate 16g
Fibre 3g

○ Total Fat 4g
Saturated Fat <1g
Polyunsaturated Fat <1g
Monounsaturated Fat 3g

○ Cholesterol 0mg

○ Sodium 113mg

Preparation Time: 15 minutes, plus 1 hour chilling
Serves: 4

CELERIAC & CARROT SALAD

200g (7oz) celeriac, finely grated
200g (7oz) carrots, finely grated

FOR THE DRESSING
juice of 1 orange and 1 tsp grated zest
juice of ½ lemon

2 tsp Dijon mustard
1 tbsp olive oil
2 tbsp sultanas or raisins, soaked in a little orange juice for 20 minutes
salt and freshly ground black pepper, to taste

Mix together the dressing ingredients, and pour over the celeriac and carrots. Refrigerate for about 1 hour before serving.

EACH SERVING PROVIDES:

○ Calories 100

○ Protein 2g

○ Carbohydrate 13g
Fibre 3g

○ Total Fat 4g
Saturated Fat <1g
Polyunsaturated Fat <1g
Monounsaturated Fat 3g

○ Cholesterol 0mg

○ Sodium 134mg

Preparation Time: 15 minutes, plus 1 hour standing
Serves: 4

EACH SERVING PROVIDES:

○ Calories 170

○ Protein 17g

○ Carbohydrate 15g
 Fibre 4g

○ Total Fat 5g
 Saturated Fat 1g
 Polyunsaturated Fat 1g
 Monounsaturated Fat 3g

○ Cholesterol 26mg

○ Sodium 330mg

BUYING TIP

Try to avoid tuna canned in oil or brine. Tuna in spring water has much lower levels of fat and salt.

Preparation Time: 7 minutes, plus 1 hour chilling
Serves: 4

TUNA & BEAN SALAD

BASED ON AN ITALIAN CLASSIC, THIS SALAD IS A SUCCESSFUL MARRIAGE

OF LOW-FAT, HIGH-FIBRE BEANS, FRESH HERBS, RED ONION, AND

FLAKES OF TUNA. SERVE IT AS A MAIN COURSE, IF DESIRED, WITH

A CHUNK OF SEEDED WHOLEMEAL BREAD.

200g (7oz) canned tuna chunks in spring water
220g (7½oz) canned flageolet beans or butter beans, in water
1 red onion, sliced into paper-thin rings
1 clove garlic, crushed
1 dessert apple, cored and chopped
1 red pepper, cored, deseeded, and finely chopped
4 tbsp chopped fresh flat-leaf parsley

FOR THE DRESSING
3 tbsp fat-free Greek yogurt
2 tsp honey mustard, or 1 tsp English mustard mixed with 2 tsp honey
1 tbsp extra-virgin olive oil
2 tbsp white wine vinegar, or lemon or lime juice
salt and freshly ground black pepper, to taste

1 Mix together the dressing ingredients until combined.

2 Pour the dressing over the salad ingredients in a large serving bowl, and refrigerate for about 1 hour to allow the flavours to develop.

VARIATION
Chicken and Chick-pea Salad Replace the tuna, beans, and apple with 300g (10oz) grilled, skinless, boneless chicken breast, sliced, 220g (7½oz) canned chick-peas, and 1 pear, cored and chopped.

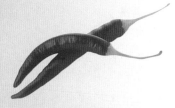

Smoky Aubergine & Tomato Salad

AUBERGINES ARE LOW IN CALORIES, BUT THEY HAVE AN ABILITY

TO ABSORB OIL THAT CAN SERIOUSLY BUMP UP THEIR CALORIE COUNT.

GRILLING OR BAKING THEM KEEPS THEIR FAT CONTENT DOWN.

500g (1lb) aubergines
350g (11½oz) tomatoes, skinned, deseeded, and chopped
1 small red onion or 4 spring onions, finely chopped
1 clove garlic, crushed
2 tbsp extra-virgin olive oil
juice of 1 lemon and 1 tsp grated zest
1–2 red or green chillies, deseeded and finely chopped
3 tbsp chopped fresh parsley, mint, or sweet marjoram,
or a combination of the three
salt and freshly ground black pepper, to taste

1 Preheat the oven to maximum. Bake the aubergines whole for 20–25 minutes, until the skin is evenly charred and the flesh is soft. With a sharp knife make a deep cut in each aubergine, then place the aubergines in a colander to cool slightly.

2 Scoop out the aubergine flesh with a spoon, then coarsely chop and return it to the cleaned colander. Cover, and leave to drain for at least 1 hour to remove any bitter juices and excess moisture. (To speed up this process, gently squeeze the aubergine flesh before draining to extract as much moisture as possible.)

3 Finely chop the aubergine flesh until it is almost puréed but still retains some texture. Add the rest of the ingredients, and mix well. Season, and refrigerate for about 1 hour before serving.

VARIATION

Smoky Aubergine and Tahini Salad Omit the tomatoes and oil. Mix together 4 tablespoons of light tahini and 3 tablespoons of water. Add the mixture to the rest of the ingredients in step 3, above. Season, mix well, and refrigerate for about 1 hour before serving.

★ STAR INGREDIENT
Chillies are a rich source of the antioxidant vitamin C, which may help to neutralize cell damage caused by free radicals.

EACH SERVING PROVIDES:

○ Calories 110

○ Protein 2g

○ Carbohydrate 7g
Fibre 4g

○ Total Fat 8g
Saturated Fat 1g
Polyunsaturated Fat 1g
Monounsaturated Fat 6g

○ Cholesterol 0mg

○ Sodium 13mg

SERVING TIP
For a smooth dip, purée the aubergine flesh in a food processor or blender.

Preparation Time: 35 minutes, plus 1 hour draining, and 1 hour chilling
Serves: 4

MARINATED & GRILLED OYSTER MUSHROOMS

ASIAN MUSHROOMS – SHIITAKE, OYSTER, OR BLACK TREE FUNGUS – ARE

REPUTED TO REDUCE CHOLESTEROL LEVELS IN THE BODY, HELPING

TO LESSEN THE RISK OF STROKES AND HEART ATTACKS.

500g (1lb) large oyster mushrooms, trimmed
2 tbsp finely chopped fresh thyme, to garnish

FOR THE MARINADE
1 tbsp toasted sesame oil
2.5cm (1in) piece of fresh ginger, grated
2 shallots, finely chopped
2 cloves garlic, crushed
1 red chilli, deseeded and finely chopped
4 tbsp rice wine or dry sherry
1–2 tsp honey or sugar

1 Mix together the ingredients for the marinade. Pour the marinade over the mushrooms, and leave to marinate for 1–2 hours, occasionally turning the mushrooms in the liquid.

2 Heat the grill to high, and grill the mushrooms, gill-side up, for 8–10 minutes, occasionally basting them with the marinade, until the mushroom are just cooked and tender.

3 Place the mushrooms in a serving dish. Spoon over the remaining marinade and grill-pan juices, and serve sprinkled with the thyme.

VARIATION
Marinated and Grilled Tofu Replace the mushrooms with 350g (11½oz) tofu, cut into thick slices. Serve sprinkled with 4 spring onions, trimmed and finely shredded, instead of the fresh thyme.

★ STAR INGREDIENT
Mushrooms, particularly oriental varieties, contain compounds that are reputed to stimulate the immune system.

EACH SERVING PROVIDES:

○ Calories 60

○ Protein 2g

○ Carbohydrate 4g
Fibre <1g

○ Total Fat 4g
Saturated Fat 1g
Polyunsaturated Fat 2g
Monounsaturated Fat 1g

○ Cholesterol 0mg

○ Sodium 100mg

SERVING TIPS
Serve this delicious, simple dish as an accompaniment to roast or grilled chicken, or as a vegetarian main course with noodles or rice.

Preparation Time: 15 minutes, plus 1–2 hours marinating
Serves: 4

APPLE & CABBAGE SALAD

A REFRESHING AND LIGHT VERSION OF SAUERKRAUT, THIS SWEET-SOUR

WARM SALAD FEATURES A HEALTHY COMBINATION OF ONIONS,

APPLE, AND CABBAGE. IT CAN BE SERVED ON ITS OWN, WITH PASTA,

OR WITH GRAINS SUCH AS BULGAR, RICE, OR BARLEY.

✱ STAR INGREDIENT

Savoy cabbage is rich in beta-carotene, an antioxidant that may help to prevent cell damage by free radicals.

EACH SERVING PROVIDES:

○ Calories 90

○ Protein 4g

○ Carbohydrate 16g
 Fibre 5g

○ Total Fat 3g
 Saturated Fat 1g
 Polyunsaturated Fat 1g
 Monounsaturated Fat 1g

○ Cholesterol 0mg

○ Sodium 10mg

Preparation Time: 30 minutes
Serves: 4

2 onions, finely sliced
6 tbsp apple juice
6 tbsp cider vinegar
1 tsp olive or grapeseed oil
2 tsp black or yellow mustard seeds,
 roasted in a dry frying pan
1 small Savoy cabbage, trimmed, cored,
 and finely shredded
2 dessert apples, cored, and finely diced
salt and freshly ground black pepper, to taste

1 Place the onions, apple juice, and half the vinegar in a wok or a large frying pan. Bring to a boil, then reduce the heat, and simmer for 8–10 minutes, until most of the liquid has evaporated. Increase the heat, add the oil and mustard seeds, and cook, stirring continuously, for 4–5 minutes, until the onions start to brown.

2 Add the cabbage, apples, and the remaining vinegar. Stir-fry for 2 minutes, or until the cabbage has started to wilt. Season, cover, and steam over a low heat for 5–8 minutes, until the cabbage is tender but still retains a slight crunch. Remove the lid, increase the heat, and boil until most of the liquid has evaporated.

VARIATIONS

Chinese Cabbage and Pear Salad Replace the Savoy cabbage and apple with Chinese cabbage, finely shredded, and 2 ripe pears, cored and finely diced.

Pineapple and Cabbage Salad Replace the apple juice with pineapple juice. Replace the apples with 1 small pineapple, peeled, cored, and finely chopped.

Spring Vegetables with Oriental Dressing

STEAMING IS THE BEST WAY TO PRESERVE THE SWEET FLAVOUR

OF VEGETABLES AND TO RETAIN WATER-SOLUBLE VITAMINS THAT

CAN BE LOST DURING BOILING.

*500g (1lb) mixed vegetables, such as broccoli, mangetout,
baby carrots, and courgettes*

For the Dressing
4 spring onions, finely chopped
2.5cm (1in) piece of fresh ginger, finely chopped
1 clove garlic, finely chopped
1 chilli, deseeded and finely chopped (optional)
4 tbsp mirin
2 tbsp rice wine vinegar or cider vinegar
1 tbsp sesame oil
1 tbsp sesame seeds, roasted in a dry frying pan

1 Steam the vegetables for 4–5 minutes, until just tender.

2 Mix together the ingredients for the dressing, and pour over the warm vegetables. Leave the vegetables to marinate for at least 10 minutes, turning them frequently, to allow the flavours to develop.

Variation
Winter Vegetables with Oriental Dressing Replace the spring vegetables with the same quantity of Brussels sprouts, red cabbage, and carrots. Use 1 teaspoon poppy seeds, roasted in a dry frying pan, instead of the sesame seeds.

✳ STAR INGREDIENT
Mangetout contain useful amounts of the antioxidants vitamin C and beta-carotene, as well as fibre, which may lower cholesterol levels in the body.

EACH SERVING PROVIDES:

○ Calories 90

○ Protein 4g

○ Carbohydrate 5g
 Fibre 3g

○ Total Fat 7g
 Saturated Fat 1g
 Polyunsaturated Fat 3g
 Monounsaturated Fat 2g

○ Cholesterol 0mg

○ Sodium 15mg

BUYING TIP
Mirin is a sweet Japanese wine made from rice. It can be found in oriental shops and some supermarkets.

Preparation Time: 10 minutes, plus 10 minutes marinating
Serves: 4

Red peppers contain plentiful amounts of the antioxidants vitamin C and beta-carotene, as well as some vitamin E.

EACH SERVING PROVIDES:

○ Calories 60

○ Protein 3g

○ Carbohydrate 12g
 Fibre 2g

○ Total Fat <1g
 Saturated Fat <1g
 Polyunsaturated Fat <1g
 Monounsaturated Fat <1g

○ Cholesterol 0mg

○ Sodium 6mg

SERVING TIPS
The grilled vegetables are delicious as an accompaniment to grilled meat or fish, or as a main dish with rice or pasta.

Preparation Time: 25 minutes, plus 1 hour marinating
Serves: 4

MEDITERRANEAN GRIDDLED VEGETABLE SALAD

THIS LOW-FAT ADAPTATION OF A FAVOURITE MEDITERRANEAN RECIPE FEATURES BRIGHTLY COLOURED PEPPERS AND FRESH CITRUS JUICE, BOTH OF WHICH ARE FULL OF BENEFICIAL ANTIOXIDANTS.

2 red peppers, cored, deseeded, and quartered
1 small aubergine, sliced
2 courgettes, sliced
salt and freshly ground black pepper, to taste
fresh basil leaves, to garnish

FOR THE MARINADE
juice of 2 oranges and 1 tsp grated orange zest
juice of 1 lemon
1 tbsp olive oil
1 clove garlic, crushed

1 To make the marinade, mix together the orange juice and zest, lemon juice, olive oil, and garlic in a non-corrosive dish. Add the vegetables, turning them in the marinade, then leave to marinate for about 1 hour. Remove the vegetables from the marinade and drain well, reserving the marinade.

2 Heat a griddle and brush it with a little of the marinade. Cook the vegetables for about 3–4 minutes on each side, until just tender and blackened but still crisp, then keep hot.

3 Place the marinade in a small saucepan and bring to a boil. Boil rapidly until the liquid has reduced to about 3–4 tablespoons. Pour the marinade over the warm vegetables, and mix. Leave to cool to room temperature. Season, and sprinkle with the basil leaves before serving.

★ STAR INGREDIENT

Mangoes are a rich source of the antioxidant beta-carotene. It has been shown that those who eat more antioxidant-rich foods are less prone to heart disease.

EACH SERVING PROVIDES:

○ Calories 170

○ Protein 2g

○ Carbohydrate 43g
   Fibre 3g

○ Total Fat <0.5g
   Saturated Fat <0.5g
   Polyunsaturated Fat <0.5g
   Monounsaturated Fat <0.5g

○ Cholesterol 0mg

○ Sodium 36mg

PREPARATION TIP

You can prepare the sorbet in advance and store it in the freezer for up to a month.

Preparation Time: 15 minutes, plus 4½ hours freezing
Serves: 4

MANGO WATER ICE

A HEALTHIER, VIRTUALLY FAT-FREE ALTERNATIVE TO DAIRY ICE CREAM, WATER ICES MAKE A WONDERFULLY REFRESHING END TO A MEAL. OTHER PULPY FRUITS CAN BE USED INSTEAD OF THE MANGOES.

2 large mangoes, peeled, stoned, and chopped
juice of 1 lemon
100ml (3½fl oz) mango juice
2 egg whites
100g (3½oz) caster sugar
fresh fruits, such as nectarines, mango,
or pineapple, to decorate

1 Place the mangoes, lemon juice, and mango juice in a food processor, and blend until smooth. Transfer the mango purée to a freezer container, cover, and freeze for 45 minutes. Remove the mango purée from the freezer and beat, until almost smooth. Return to the freezer for 45 minutes, or until partly frozen.

2 Place the egg whites in a bowl and whisk to form soft peaks. Continue to whisk while gradually adding half the sugar. Whisk until the mixture forms long peaks, then fold in the remaining sugar.

3 Transfer the mango purée to a food processor. Whisk to break down the ice crystals and, with the machine running, gradually add the egg-white mixture, a tablespoonful at a time. Blend until the mixture turns into a soft slush. Return the mixture to the container, cover, and freeze for 3 hours, or until frozen. Serve decorated with the fresh fruits.

DESSERTS *These low-fat desserts will satisfy the sweetest tooth and a wide range of tastes. The vibrant mango sorbet and the tangy pear yogurt ice will refresh the palate, while the sweet polenta gnocchi and the meringue pie are perfect comfort puddings.*

PEAR YOGURT ICE

THIS DELICIOUSLY PERFUMED AND REFRESHING LOW-FAT ICE MAKES AN IDEAL CONCLUSION TO A SUMMER LUNCH OR SUPPER. SOFT FRUITS, SUCH AS RASPBERRIES, STRAWBERRIES, OR BLACKBERRIES, ARE PERFECT ALTERNATIVES TO THE PEARS.

* **STAR INGREDIENT**

Pears are low in fat and contain soluble fibre, vitamin C, and potassium, a combination that may help to lower cholesterol levels and regulate blood pressure.

EACH SERVING PROVIDES:

○ Calories 130

○ Protein 6g

○ Carbohydrate 27g
Fibre 2g

○ Total Fat <0.5g
Saturated Fat <0.5g
Polyunsaturated Fat <0.5g
Monounsaturated Fat <0.5g

○ Cholesterol 0mg

○ Sodium 54mg

SERVING TIP

Allow frozen desserts to stand at room temperature or in the bottom of the refrigerator for 30 minutes before serving.

Preparation Time: 40 minutes, plus 3 hours freezing
Serves: 4

6 tbsp water
juice of 1 lemon
1 tbsp honey
1 vanilla pod, halved and seeds scraped out
400g (13oz) ripe pears, peeled, cored, and quartered
200ml (7fl oz) fat-free Greek yogurt
1 egg white
3 tbsp caster sugar

1 Place the water, lemon juice, honey, and vanilla pod and seeds in a non-corrosive saucepan. Add the pears and bring to a boil. Reduce the heat, cover, and simmer for 20 minutes, or until the pears are tender.

2 Using a slotted spoon, lift out the pears and put them in a food processor. Remove the vanilla pod, then boil the cooking liquid until reduced to 4 tablespoons. Add the liquid to the pears, and blend into a smooth purée. Add the yogurt and blend. Spoon the mixture into a freezer container, then leave to cool. Cover, and freeze for 1–1½ hours, until almost frozen, but still soft in the centre.

3 Place the egg white in a bowl, and whisk to form soft peaks. Continue to whisk, while gradually adding half the sugar, until the mixture forms long peaks, then fold in the remaining sugar.

4 Transfer the semi-frozen yogurt mixture to a food processor. Whisk until soft and smooth. Fold in the egg-white mixture, then transfer to the container and freeze for 1½ hours, or until frozen.

✱ STAR INGREDIENT
Strawberries are rich in fibre and vitamin C and also contain ellagic acid, a reputed protector against the harmful effects of tobacco smoke and pollutants.

EACH SERVING PROVIDES:

○ Calories 220

○ Protein 9g

○ Carbohydrate 43g
 Fibre 3g

○ Total Fat <1g
 Saturated Fat <0.5g
 Polyunsaturated Fat <1g
 Monounsaturated Fat <1g

○ Cholesterol 0mg

○ Sodium 77mg

Preparation Time: 15 minutes, plus 3–4 hours draining and 1 hour chilling.
Serves: 4

LAYERED FRUIT & YOGURT MOUSSE

FRESH FRUITS ARE STEEPED IN A CITRUS JUICE AND ORANGE LIQUEUR
MARINADE, THEN LAYERED WITH A SOFT AND FLUFFY YOGURT
MOUSSE TO MAKE THIS LIGHT, MELT-IN-THE-MOUTH DESSERT.

juice of 1 lemon and grated zest of ½ lemon
juice of 1 orange and grated zest of ½ orange
3 tbsp orange liqueur or brandy
pulp of 3 passion fruits
4 kiwi fruit, peeled and cut into bite-sized cubes
150g (5oz) strawberries, hulled and quartered
150g (5oz) white grapes, halved

FOR THE MOUSSE
200g (7oz) fat-free Greek yogurt or fromage frais
1 tbsp lemon juice and ½ tsp grated lemon zest
2 tsp orange flower water
2 egg whites
6 tbsp caster sugar
½ tsp raspberry vinegar

1 To make the yogurt mousse, beat the yogurt with the lemon juice and zest, and orange flower water.

2 Whisk together the egg whites, half the sugar, and the raspberry vinegar to form stiff peaks, then gently fold in the remaining sugar. Fold the egg-white mixture into the yogurt mixture. Line a sieve with a piece of muslin or cheesecloth. Stand the sieve over a bowl, then spoon in the yogurt mixture. Cover, and leave to drain in the refrigerator for 3–4 hours, until slightly firm.

3 In a large bowl, mix together the citrus juices and zest, orange liqueur, and passion fruit pulp. Add the kiwi fruit, strawberries, and grapes, reserving a few to decorate. Cover, and refrigerate for at least 1 hour. To serve, spoon alternate layers of the marinated fruits and the yogurt mousse in 4 tall glasses. Decorate with the reserved grapes.

FIGS WITH MARBLED YOGURT & HONEY SAUCE

FIGS MAKE THE IDEAL LOW-FAT DESSERT – SOFT, SWEET, AND

SENSUOUS – WHILE HONEY CAN BE USED TO ADD

A LITTLE EXTRA LUXURY TO NATURAL YOGURT.

12 ripe figs
200g (7oz) fat-free Greek yogurt, chilled
1–2 tbsp chopped fresh mint, plus sprigs to decorate (optional)
3 tbsp clear honey

1 Slice each fig into quarters, leaving them attached at the stem end. Arrange the figs on 4 chilled plates, then press each fig gently until it fans out slightly.

2 Spoon the yogurt into a bowl and stir in the mint. Drizzle the honey over the top and carefully fold it in. Add a spoonful of the yogurt sauce to each serving, and decorate with a sprig of mint, if using.

EACH SERVING PROVIDES:
- Calories 160
- Protein 8g
- Carbohydrate 34g
  Fibre 3g
- Total Fat <1g
  Saturated Fat <0.5g
  Polyunsaturated Fat <1g
  Monounsaturated Fat <1g
- Cholesterol 0mg
- Sodium 43mg

Preparation Time: 5 minutes
Serves: 4

MIXED MELON SALAD

1 small Galia melon, deseeded
1 small Honeydew melon, deseeded
1 small Charentais melon, deseeded
1 tbsp chopped fresh mint

2 tbsp kirsch or apricot liqueur
1 small watermelon, deseeded
2 tbsp clear honey

1 With a melon baller, scoop out the flesh from the melons, apart from the watermelon, into neat balls. Scatter the mint and sprinkle the kirsch over the melon balls. Cover, and refrigerate for at least 1 hour.

2 Scoop out the watermelon flesh, removing any seeds, and place it in a food processor. Add the honey and blend into a smooth purée. Cover, and refrigerate for at least 1 hour. To serve, divide the watermelon sauce between 4 plates, then arrange the melon balls on top. Spoon the marinade over the melon and serve.

EACH SERVING PROVIDES:
- Calories 200
- Protein 3g
- Carbohydrate 43g
  Fibre 3g
- Total Fat 1g
  Saturated Fat <1g
  Polyunsaturated Fat <1g
  Monounsaturated Fat <1g
- Cholesterol 0mg
- Sodium 87mg

Preparation Time: 15 minutes, plus 2 hours chilling
Serves: 4

EACH SERVING PROVIDES:

◯ Calories 100

◯ Protein 1g

◯ Carbohydrate 23g
  Fibre 3g

◯ Total Fat 0.5g
  Saturated Fat 0g
  Polyunsaturated Fat <0.5g
  Monounsaturated Fat <0.5g

◯ Cholesterol 0mg

◯ Sodium 7mg

Preparation Time: 25 minutes,
plus 10 minutes cooling
Serves: 4

POACHED SPICED PEARS

THAT IS MY IDEA OF HEAVEN – TENDER, JUICY PEARS POACHED

IN A LIGHT, PERFUMED RED WINE.

500ml (17fl oz) full-bodied, fruity red wine
2–3 tbsp clear honey
4 cardamom pods, crushed
juice and grated zest of 1 lemon
1 small cinnamon stick
1 tsp black peppercorns
4 ripe pears, peeled, with the stems attached
sprigs of fresh mint, to decorate

1 Combine the wine, honey, cardamom, lemon juice and zest, cinnamon, and peppercorns in a large, non-corrosive saucepan. Bring to a boil, reduce the heat, skim away any froth, and simmer for 5 minutes.

2 Add the pears and poach gently for 10–15 minutes, until tender. Remove from the heat and leave to cool. Strain the cooking liquid. Serve the pears in 4 bowls with a little of the cooking liquid. Decorate each serving with a sprig of mint.

EACH SERVING PROVIDES:

◯ Calories 180

◯ Protein 2g

◯ Carbohydrate 46g
  Fibre 2g

◯ Total Fat 0.5g
  Saturated Fat 0g
  Polyunsaturated Fat <0.5g
  Monounsaturated Fat <0.5g

◯ Cholesterol 0mg

◯ Sodium 6mg

Preparation Time: 30 minutes,
plus 30 minutes marinating
Serves: 4

BAKED BANANAS WITH VANILLA

3 tbsp sultanas
3 tbsp rum
2 tbsp soft dark brown sugar
or molasses

juice and grated zest of 1 small lemon
4 bananas, thickly sliced
1 vanilla pod, sliced lengthways into
quarters

1 Combine the sultanas, rum, sugar, and lemon juice and zest in a bowl. Stir in the bananas. Cover, and leave to marinate for 30 minutes.

2 Preheat the oven to 220°C/425°F/Gas 7. Divide the banana mixture between 4 x 20cm (8in) foil rounds, placing it in a small pile in the centre of each one. Fold each foil round into a loose parcel, but do not close the top. Add a quarter of the vanilla pod and a little of the marinating liquid to each parcel. Close tightly, and bake for 20 minutes, until the bananas have softened. Serve the bananas in their foil parcels.

✱ STAR INGREDIENTS

Fresh fruits contain beneficial amounts of antioxidant vitamins and soluble fibre.

EACH SERVING PROVIDES:

○ Calories 120

○ Protein 2g

○ Carbohydrate 25g
  Fibre 1g

○ Total Fat 2g
  Saturated Fat <1g
  Polyunsaturated Fat <1g
  Monounsaturated Fat 1g

○ Cholesterol 0mg

○ Sodium 68mg

PREPARATION TIP

You can prepare the meringue base in advance and store it in an airtight container for a few days before use.

Preparation Time: 1 hour, 10 minutes, plus 30 minutes cooling
Serves: 6–8

PASSION FRUIT PAVLOVA

THIS IMPRESSIVE, LIGHT, AND INDULGENT DESSERT COULD GRACE THE TABLE OF ANY ELEGANT DINNER PARTY. YET IT IS NOT AS NAUGHTY AS IT LOOKS: FRESH FRUITS AND ORANGE JUICE ARE EXCELLENT SOURCES OF VITAMIN C AND BETA-CAROTENE.

3 egg whites
1 tsp cream of tartar or 1 tsp raspberry vinegar
100g (3½oz) caster sugar
2 tsp cornflour or potato flour

FOR THE TOPPING
pulp of 6 passion fruits
150ml (¼ pint) fresh orange juice
2 tbsp caster sugar
2 tbsp arrowroot, dissolved in 2 tbsp orange juice
30g (1oz) half-fat unsalted butter
fresh seasonal fruits and mint leaves, to decorate

1 Preheat the oven to 150°C/300°F/Gas 2. Line a baking sheet with baking parchment. In a large bowl, whisk together the egg whites and cream of tartar until they form stiff peaks. Gradually whisk in half the sugar, then fold in the remaining sugar and the cornflour until the mixture forms long peaks.

2 Spoon the mixture into a 20cm (8in) round on the prepared baking sheet lined with parchment. Bake for 1 hour, or until pale biscuit in colour. Turn off the oven, and leave the meringue to cool.

3 To make the topping, place the passion fruit pulp, orange juice, and sugar in a small pan. Bring to a boil, then reduce the heat, and simmer for 15 minutes, or until reduced by half. Add the prepared arrowroot mixture and boil for 1 minute, or until thickened. Remove the mixture from the heat and beat in the butter. Leave to cool.

4 Pour the topping on to the meringue base. Decorate with the fresh fruits and mint leaves, and chill before serving.

PEACH & GINGER MERINGUE PIE

ANY POACHED FRUITS CAN BE USED IN THIS LOW-FAT ALTERNATIVE

TO LEMON MERINGUE PIE, BUT THEY MUST BE

SUCCULENT AND FULLY RIPE. SERVE THE PIE WARM OR COLD

WITH A SPOONFUL OF FAT-FREE YOGURT.

★ STAR INGREDIENT

Peaches are rich in nutrients, including fibre, potassium, and vitamin C. Like almost all other fruits, they contain no cholesterol.

EACH SERVING PROVIDES:

○ Calories 175

○ Protein 4g

○ Carbohydrate 41g
Fibre 2g

○ Total Fat <0.5g
Saturated Fat <0.5g
Polyunsaturated Fat <0.5g
Monounsaturated Fat <0.5g

○ Cholesterol 0mg

○ Sodium 50mg

PREPARATION TIP

Canned peaches in natural juice can be used instead of the fresh fruit, if preferred.

Preparation Time: 45 minutes
Serves: 4

4 large peaches
150ml (¼ pint) white wine
2 tbsp lemon juice and grated zest of 1 lemon
1 stick lemongrass, peeled and halved
1 tbsp clear honey or caster sugar
3 egg whites
1 tsp raspberry vinegar
100g (3½oz) caster sugar
40g (1½oz) stem ginger, finely chopped

1 Place the peaches in boiling water for 1 minute. Refresh them in cold water, then halve, stone, and peel them. Place the wine, lemon juice and zest, lemongrass, and honey in a non-corrosive saucepan. Bring to a boil, then reduce the heat, skimming away any froth, and simmer for 5 minutes.

2 Preheat the oven to 200°C/400°F/Gas 6. Return the peaches to the saucepan and poach for 8 minutes, or until just tender. Using a slotted spoon, lift out the peaches, and set aside. Strain the cooking liquid, discarding the lemon zest and lemongrass. Return the liquid to the saucepan, then bring to a rapid boil. Boil for 5–6 minutes, until the liquid has reduced and is syrupy and glossy.

3 Whisk together the egg whites and raspberry vinegar, until they form soft peaks. Gradually whisk in half the sugar, then fold in the remaining sugar and the stem ginger, until the mixture forms long peaks.

4 Arrange the peaches in a 20cm (8in) pie dish. Pour the cooking liquid over the peaches, and spoon the meringue mixture over the top. Bake for 15–20 minutes, until the top is crisp and golden.

APPLE & RASPBERRY CRUMBLE

IN THIS NEW TAKE ON THE TRADITIONAL CRUMBLE, FRESH APPLES
AND SOFT BERRIES ARE BAKED UNDER A CRUNCHY
GRANOLA TOPPING OF OATS AND HONEY. A SPOONFUL OF FAT-FREE
NATURAL YOGURT ADDS THE FINISHING TOUCH.

★ STAR INGREDIENT
Raspberries are abundant in nutrients, such as vitamins C and E, zinc, potassium, and folate.

EACH SERVING PROVIDES:

○ Calories 220

○ Protein 4g

○ Carbohydrate 48g
  Fibre 4g

○ Total Fat 2g
  Saturated Fat <1g
  Polyunsaturated Fat <1g
  Monounsaturated Fat <1g

○ Cholesterol 0mg

○ Sodium 15mg

PREPARATION TIP
Other fruits, such as plums, rhubarb, blackberries, or peaches, can be used in this dessert.

Preparation Time: 45 minutes
Serves: 6

*6 dessert apples, peeled, cored,
and coarsely chopped*
75g (3oz) raisins
juice of ½ lemon
*150ml (¼ pint) dry white wine
or apple juice*
4 cloves
4 tbsp clear honey
150g (5oz) rolled oats
100g (3½oz) raspberries
1 tsp ground cinnamon

1 Preheat the oven to 220°C/425°F/Gas 7. Place the apples, raisins, lemon juice, wine, cloves, and 1 tablespoon of the honey in a saucepan. Bring to a boil, then reduce the heat, and simmer for 8–10 minutes, or until the apples are just soft.

2 Remove the apples using a slotted spoon, and place them in a 20cm (8in) pie dish. Bring the cooking liquid to a boil, then boil for 5 minutes, until it has reduced by two-thirds. Pour the liquid over the apples in the pie dish.

3 In a small saucepan, warm the rest of the honey for 2 minutes, until melted. Mix in the oats and cook for a further 4–5 minutes, until the mixture is crisp and golden.

4 Scatter the raspberries over the apples, and cover with an even layer of the oat mixture. Sprinkle with cinnamon and bake for 15 minutes, or until the crumble has browned and is crisp. Serve hot or warm.

MIXED BERRIES WITH SWEET POLENTA GNOCCHI

THIS ATTRACTIVE DESSERT FEATURES VITAMIN-RICH FRESH BERRIES SERVED WITH GOLDEN SULTANA POLENTA GNOCCHI. THE GNOCCHI ARE BEST SERVED WHEN STILL WARM.

300g (10oz) mixed berries, such as strawberries, blueberries, and raspberries
4 tbsp Grand Marnier or brandy
juice of 1 orange
icing sugar, to dust

FOR THE GNOCCHI
250ml (8fl oz) water
juice of 1 lemon
3 tbsp caster sugar
15g (½oz) half-fat unsalted butter
5 tbsp instant polenta or semolina
1 tsp grated lemon zest
75g (3oz) sultanas, soaked in a little hot water or orange juice for 20 minutes

1 Sprinkle the berries with the Grand Marnier and orange juice, and leave to marinate for 1 hour.

2 Line a baking sheet with baking parchment. To make the gnocchi, place the water, lemon juice, sugar, and butter in a saucepan, and bring to a boil. Reduce the heat and gradually whisk in the polenta. Cook, stirring frequently, for 5 minutes, until thickened and creamy.

3 Remove from the heat and stir in the lemon zest and sultanas, discarding the orange juice. Using a spatula dipped in cold water, spread the polenta into an even, smooth layer, about 1cm (½in) thick, on the prepared baking sheet. Leave to cool and set. Cut the polenta into 4 triangles. Heat a griddle or skillet and cook the polenta over a medium-high heat for 1–2 minutes on each side, until golden.

4 Transfer the berries with their marinating liquid to 4 plates, and serve with the polenta gnocchi. Decorate with a dusting of icing sugar.

✶ STAR INGREDIENT
Blueberries contain valuable amounts of fibre, vitamin C, and B vitamins. They also feature flavonoids that may improve the circulation and aid the body's defences against infection.

EACH SERVING PROVIDES:

○ Calories 220

○ Protein 3g

○ Carbohydrate 42g
  Fibre 2g

○ Total Fat 2g
  Saturated Fat 1g
  Polyunsaturated Fat <1g
  Monounsaturated Fat <1g

○ Cholesterol 5mg

○ Sodium 26mg

PREPARATION TIP
The polenta triangles can be made the day before and stored in the refrigerator until ready to use.

Preparation Time: 30 minutes, plus 1 hour marinating
Serves: 4

CARAMELIZED PINEAPPLE

✱ STAR INGREDIENT
Pineapples contain useful amounts of magnesium, zinc, and fibre, as well as antioxidants, which may neutralize cell damage by free radicals.

EACH SERVING PROVIDES:

○ Calories 255

○ Protein 2g

○ Carbohydrate 65g
Fibre 4g

○ Total Fat <1g
Saturated Fat 0g
Polyunsaturated Fat <1g
Monounsaturated Fat <1g

○ Cholesterol 0mg

○ Sodium 11mg

PREPARATION TIP
Canned pineapple can be used instead of fresh, but choose fruit that is preserved in natural juice rather than syrup.

Preparation Time: 40 minutes, plus 1 hour chilling
Serves: 4

NUMEROUS STUDIES HAVE REVEALED THAT BROMELAIN ENZYMES, WHICH ARE FOUND IN PINEAPPLES, AID DIGESTION. THIS SIMPLE DESSERT MAKES THE PERFECT END TO A MEAL, AND IS DELICIOUS WITH A SPOONFUL OF LOW-FAT FROMAGE FRAIS.

2 pineapples, peeled and cored
4 tbsp rum or kirsch
2 tbsp sweet white wine, water, or fruit juice
1 vanilla pod, halved lengthways, and seeds scraped out
100g (3½oz) caster sugar
1 tbsp arrowroot or cornflour, dissolved in 2 tbsp of wine, water, or fruit juice
30g (1oz) stem ginger, finely chopped
100g (3½oz) strawberries, raspberries, or blueberries, to decorate

1 Slice one of the pineapples into 8 rings, then place the rings in a shallow bowl. Pour 2 tablespoons of the rum over the pineapple, and turn the fruit in the liquid. Cover, and leave to marinate for 30 minutes.

2 Roughly chop the other pineapple. Place the fruit in a non-corrosive saucepan. Add the wine, the vanilla pod and seeds, and 75g (2½oz) of the sugar, then stir well. Bring to a boil, then reduce the heat, and simmer for 20 minutes, or until the pineapple is tender.

3 Remove the vanilla pod, then transfer the cooked pineapple to a blender or food processor. Blend for 1–2 minutes, until smooth. Return the pineapple to the pan with the vanilla pod and bring to a boil. Reduce the heat, then stir in the arrowroot mixture. Simmer for a further 1–2 minutes, stirring occasionally, until the pineapple sauce has thickened, then leave to cool. Stir in the stem ginger and the remaining rum. Cover, and refrigerate for at least 1 hour.

4 Line the grill rack with foil and heat the grill to high. Place the marinated pineapple rings on the grill rack. Sprinkle with the remaining sugar and grill for 4–5 minutes on each side, or until caramelized. Arrange the pineapple rings on 4 plates, spoon over the marinade and sauce, and decorate each serving with the berries.

LIGHT CHOCOLATE MOUSSE

THIS IS A "ONCE-A-MONTH", SPECIAL TREAT – RICH, DARK, AND

INDULGENT. USE THE BEST CHOCOLATE YOU CAN FIND.

100g (3½oz) dark chocolate (at least 70 per cent
cocoa solids), broken into chunks
3 egg whites
½ tsp raspberry vinegar
100g (3½oz) caster sugar
grated zest of 1 orange
strawberries or raspberries, to decorate

1 Put the chocolate in a heat-proof bowl, placed over a saucepan of simmering water. Heat the chocolate until it melts, stirring occasionally.

2 Put the egg whites, raspberry vinegar, and sugar in a heat-proof bowl, placed over a pan of barely simmering water. Whisk the mixture, preferably with an electric hand whisk, for 5–8 minutes, until stiff.

3 Remove the egg-white mixture from the heat, then gently fold in the melted chocolate, making sure that it is thoroughly blended. Pour the mixture into 4 ramekins. Leave to cool, then refrigerate for at least 2 hours. Decorate with strawberries, and serve.

EACH SERVING PROVIDES:

- ○ Calories 235
- ○ Protein 3g
- ○ Carbohydrate 42g
  Fibre 1g
- ○ Total Fat 7g
  Saturated Fat 4g
  Polyunsaturated Fat 1g
  Monounsaturated Fat 2g
- ○ Cholesterol 2mg
- ○ Sodium 48mg

PREPARATION TIP
It is important to use the best-quality dark chocolate you can find. It should be at least 70 per cent cocoa solids.

Preparation Time: 20 minutes, plus 2 hours chilling
Serves: 4

CARAMELIZED RICE PUDDING

4 tbsp caster sugar
1 tbsp lemon juice
575ml (18fl oz) water
200g (7oz) long-grain rice,
such as basmati or patna

15g (½oz) half-fat unsalted butter
¼ tsp saffron strands, soaked
in a little warm water
75g (3oz) raisins
1 tsp grated lemon zest

1 Place the sugar, lemon juice, and 3 tablespoons of the water in a saucepan. Cook over a high heat for 5–6 minutes, until the liquid starts to caramelize. Remove from the heat, then stir in the rice and butter.

2 Stir in the rest of the water, the saffron and its soaking water, and the raisins. Bring to a boil, then reduce the heat. Cover, and simmer for about 20 minutes, until the liquid has been absorbed and the rice is tender. Stir in the lemon zest, and serve.

EACH SERVING PROVIDES:

- ○ Calories 305
- ○ Protein 4g
- ○ Carbohydrate 69g
  Fibre 1g
- ○ Total Fat 2g
  Saturated Fat <1g
  Polyunsaturated Fat <1g
  Monounsaturated Fat 1g
- ○ Cholesterol <0.5mg
- ○ Sodium 37mg

Preparation Time: 30 minutes
Serves: 4

LOW-FAT CHINESE DIPPING SAUCE

DIP ROASTED TOFU, RAW OR LIGHTLY COOKED VEGETABLES, OR

KEBABS INTO THIS TANGY, SWEET–SOUR DIPPING SAUCE. IT IS ALSO

DELICIOUS POURED OVER GRILLED MEAT OR FISH.

1 tbsp reduced salt soy sauce
4 tbsp rice vinegar or white wine vinegar
1 clove garlic, finely chopped
1 small carrot, finely grated
1cm (½in) piece of fresh ginger, finely grated
1 tbsp caster sugar
1 small red chilli, deseeded and chopped, or ¼–½ tsp chilli powder
100ml (3½fl oz) orange or pineapple juice
1 tsp cornflour
1 spring onion, finely shredded

1 Place the soy sauce, rice vinegar, garlic, carrot, ginger, sugar, and chilli in a small, non-corrosive saucepan. Add the orange juice, reserving 1 tablespoon. Bring to a boil, then reduce the heat, and simmer for about 5 minutes, or until slightly thickened.

2 Mix together the cornflour and reserved orange juice, then stir it into the cooking liquid. Return the mixture to the boil and cook, stirring, until the sauce is thick enough to coat the back of a spoon.

3 Add the shredded spring onion, and remove from the heat. Serve either hot or at room temperature.

✴ STAR INGREDIENT
Spring onions contain compounds such as allicin, which may help to control cholesterol levels, even after a fatty meal.

TOTAL RECIPE PROVIDES:

○ Calories 60

○ Protein 1g

○ Carbohydrate 13g
Fibre 1g

○ Total Fat <0.5g
Saturated Fat <0.5g
Polyunsaturated Fat <0.5g
Monounsaturated Fat <0.5g

○ Cholesterol 0mg

○ Sodium 226mg

PREPARATION TIP
This sauce can be stored in an airtight container, in the refrigerator for up to 3 days.

Preparation Time: 15 minutes
Makes: 150ml (¼ pint)

BASICS *This diverse selection of recipes includes*

simple ideas for sauces, dressings, stocks, and accompaniments that will help you to turn the most ordinary dish into a gourmet meal, and unlike many preprepared alternatives, they are all low in fat, cholesterol, and salt.

FISH STOCK

1kg (2lb) fish bones, plus heads, and trimmings
250ml (8fl oz) dry white wine
1.5 litres (2½ pints) water
2 leeks, white part only, finely sliced
1 carrot, chopped

1 celery stick, chopped
bouquet garni, made up of 2 sprigs of thyme, 2 pieces of green leek leaves, 2 sprigs of parsley, 1 sprig of celery leaves, and 1 bay leaf
10 peppercorns
2–3 thick slices of lemon

1 Wash the fish bones, heads, and trimmings thoroughly in plenty of cold water, then drain well. Place in a large saucepan and add the wine and water. Bring to a boil, skimming away any froth.

2 Add the vegetables, bouquet garni, peppercorns, and lemon. Return to the boil, then reduce the heat, and simmer for 30 minutes, skimming the surface frequently.

3 Strain through a sieve lined with a triple layer of damp muslin, and discard the solids. Leave to cool.

VEGETABLE STOCK

I LIKE TO MAKE STOCKS USING A VARIETY OF VEGETABLES, HERBS, AND SPICES THAT REFLECT THE SEASON. TRY EXPERIMENTING WITH DIFFERENT TYPES OF FRESH PRODUCE AND FLAVOURING.

1 large onion, sliced into rings
100g (3½oz) carrots, sliced
3 cloves garlic
100g (3½oz) pumpkin, peeled, deseeded, and cubed
3 celery sticks
1 large, ripe tomato, cut into quarters
bouquet garni, made up of 4 sprigs of parsley, 4 sprigs of coriander, 2 sprigs of thyme, and 2 strips of lemon zest
1.5 litres (2½ pints) water

Place all the ingredients in a large saucepan. Bring to a boil, then reduce the heat, and simmer for 30 minutes. Strain through a sieve lined with a layer of damp muslin, and discard the solids. Leave to cool.

★ STAR INGREDIENT
Leeks provide useful amounts of iron as well as the antioxidants beta-carotene, and vitamins E and C.

PREPARATION TIP
To intensify the flavour of the stock include 1 small red mullet, while for a more delicate flavour, use only fish bones.

Preparation Time: 45 minutes
Makes: 1.5 litres (2½ pints)

PREPARATION TIPS
A chopped apple adds a delicious sweetness to this stock. In addition, 75g (3oz) okra or 2 tbsp soaked barley can thicken a stock, giving it a velvety smoothness.

Preparation Time: 45 minutes
Makes: 1.5 litres (2½ pints)

CHICKEN STOCK

STOCK CUBES CONTAIN ADDED SALT AND FAT THAT CAN BE AVOIDED

IF YOU MAKE YOUR OWN STOCK. A HOMEMADE STOCK ADDS TEXTURE

AND DEPTH TO SOUPS AND STEWS, AND WHEN REDUCED, CAN

BE USED INSTEAD OF OIL IN DRESSINGS.

✱ STAR INGREDIENT
Carrots provide rich amounts of beta-carotene and vitamin C, which have been shown to reduce blood-cholesterol levels.

PREPARATION TIP
Experiment with different flavourings, such as shallots, fresh ginger, parsley root, and celeriac.

Preparation Time: 2 hours, 45 minutes
Makes: 1.5 litres (2½ pints)

*1.5–2kg (3–4lb) chicken bones, or whole chicken,
cut into pieces*
1 leek, sliced
1 onion, unpeeled and quartered
4 carrots, coarsely chopped
2 celery sticks, coarsely chopped
*bouquet garni, made up of 3 sprigs of thyme, a few
celery leaves, 1 bay leaf, and 2–3 strips lemon zest*
4 cloves (optional)
1 tsp peppercorns (optional)
*100g (3½oz) fresh mushrooms, or 5g (1 tsp) dried
wild mushrooms, such as porcini (optional)*

1 Wash the chicken bones thoroughly in a few changes of water, then drain well. Place the bones in a large saucepan and cover with water. Bring slowly to a boil, then reduce the heat, and simmer for about 30 minutes, skimming away any froth when necessary.

2 Add the vegetables, bouquet garni, cloves, and peppercorns. Continue to simmer for about 1½–2 hours, until the liquid has reduced by about a quarter. Leave to cool slightly.

3 Strain through a sieve lined with a double layer of damp muslin, and discard the solids. Leave the stock to cool. Store refrigerated for up to 3 days, removing any traces of fat that form on the surface.

Fresh Tomato Sauce

THIS SIMPLE, VIBRANT, FRESH SAUCE CONTAINS A NUTRITIONALLY
BENEFICIAL COMBINATION OF TOMATOES, GARLIC, AND ONIONS.
IT IS DELICIOUS SPOONED OVER PASTA OR RICE, OR SERVED
AS AN ACCOMPANIMENT TO FISH OR MEAT.

2 onions, chopped
3 cloves garlic, chopped
4 tbsp water
1kg (2lb) tomatoes, coarsely chopped
1 tsp caster sugar (optional)
bouquet garni, made up of a few sprigs of celery leaves, parsley,
oregano, 1 bay leaf, and 1 strip of lemon zest (optional)
1 tbsp olive oil (optional)
salt, to taste

1 Place the onions and garlic in a heavy-based saucepan. Add the water and simmer, stirring frequently, for 5 minutes, or until the water has evaporated and the onion has softened.

2 Add the tomatoes, sugar, if using, and bouquet garni. Simmer, semi-covered, over a very low heat for 1 hour, or until the sauce has thickened. Beat in the oil, if using, and season, then simmer for a few more minutes. Press the sauce through a sieve to remove the bouquet garni and the tomato skins and seeds, and to make a smooth sauce.

Variations

Spicy Tomato Sauce Add 1–2 red chillies, deseeded and chopped, or ½ teaspoon chilli powder with the onions in step 1, above.

Tomato and Fennel Sauce For a tomato sauce to serve with fish, add 1 small fennel bulb, finely chopped, with the onions in step 1, above.

Oriental Tomato Sauce Add a 2.5cm (1in) piece of fresh ginger, finely chopped, and 2 star anise with the onions in step 1, above.

✷ STAR INGREDIENT
Tomatoes are a good source of the flavonoid quercetin, which has been shown to reduce the risk of heart disease and strokes.

TOTAL RECIPE PROVIDES:

○ Calories 380

○ Protein 8g

○ Carbohydrate 48g
Fibre 12g

○ Total Fat 20g
Saturated Fat 4g
Polyunsaturated Fat 4g
Monounsaturated Fat 12g

○ Cholesterol 0mg

○ Sodium 96mg

PREPARATION TIP
This sauce can be prepared in advance. Store it in the refrigerator, covered, for up to 3 days.

Preparation Time: 1 hour, 15 minutes
Makes: 500ml (17fl oz)

TOTAL RECIPE PROVIDES:

- ○ Calories 280
- ○ Protein 16g
- ○ Carbohydrate 56g
  Fibre 2g
- ○ Total Fat 3g
  Saturated Fat 1g
  Polyunsaturated Fat 1g
  Monounsaturated Fat 1g
- ○ Cholesterol 20mg
- ○ Sodium 240mg

Preparation Time: 25 minutes
Makes: 500ml (17fl oz)

ALMOST FAT-FREE WHITE SAUCE

2 tbsp cornflour
500ml (17fl oz) skimmed milk
1cm (½in) piece of fresh ginger, grated
50g (1½oz) shallots, finely chopped
1 clove garlic, finely chopped (optional)
2 tbsp lime or lemon juice

1 red chilli, deseeded and finely chopped (optional)
salt and freshly ground white or black pepper, to taste
a little freshly grated nutmeg, to garnish

1 Blend the cornflour with 2 tablespoons of the milk. Heat the remaining milk in a saucepan, until simmering. Add the cornflour mixture. Bring to a boil and cook for 1 minute, stirring continuously.

2 Add the ginger, shallots, garlic, lime juice, and chilli, if using. Reduce the heat, and simmer, whisking frequently, for about 15 minutes, or until the sauce is thick enough to coat the back of a spoon, then season. Serve the sauce immediately with a sprinkling of nutmeg or, if a smooth sauce is desired, sieve and reheat.

1 TABLESPOON PROVIDES:

- ○ Calories 15
- ○ Protein 2g
- ○ Carbohydrate 1g
  Fibre 0g
- ○ Total Fat <1g
  Saturated Fat <0.5g
  Polyunsaturated Fat <0.5g
  Monounsaturated Fat <0.5g
- ○ Cholesterol 0mg
- ○ Sodium 6mg

PREPARATION TIP

The low-fat spread can be kept, covered, in the refrigerator for up to 1 week.

Preparation Time: 5 minutes
Makes: 275g (9oz)

LOW-FAT SANDWICH SPREAD

THIS IS A LOW-FAT ALTERNATIVE TO BUTTER OR MARGARINE. FOR A SPREAD THAT IS EVEN LOWER IN FAT, OMIT THE OLIVE OIL.

250g (8oz) Quark
1 tbsp olive oil
1 small onion, finely grated
1 tsp sweet paprika
¼ tsp dried chilli flakes
1–2 tbsp chopped fresh parsley (optional)
½ tbsp caraway seeds (optional)
salt and freshly ground black pepper, to taste

Beat together the Quark and olive oil in a bowl. Add the remaining ingredients and seasoning, then beat well until combined.

1 TABLESPOON PROVIDES:

- ○ Calories 10
- ○ Protein <0.5g
- ○ Carbohydrate 1g
  Fibre 0g
- ○ Total Fat <1g
  Saturated Fat <1g
  Polyunsaturated Fat <1g
  Monounsaturated Fat <1g
- ○ Cholesterol 0mg
- ○ Sodium 1mg

Preparation Time: 15 minutes
Makes: 125ml (4fl oz)

FRUITY SALAD DRESSING

THIS TANGY DRESSING IS RICH IN VITAMIN C AND BETA-CAROTENE.

IT CAN BE SERVED COLD AS A SALAD DRESSING, OR HOT

AS AN ACCOMPANIMENT TO GRILLED FISH OR CHICKEN. THE

SESAME OIL GIVES IT A WONDERFUL NUTTY FLAVOUR.

250ml (8fl oz) orange or pineapple juice
juice of 1 lemon
1cm (½in) piece of fresh ginger, grated
1 tsp English mustard powder
1 tbsp dark sesame oil or virgin olive oil
salt and freshly ground black pepper, to taste

1 Place the orange juice, lemon juice, and ginger in a small, non-corrosive saucepan. Bring to a boil, skimming away any froth. Boil the mixture for about 5–8 minutes, or until glossy and syrupy.

2 Remove from the heat, then whisk in the mustard, oil, and seasoning.

1 TABLESPOON PROVIDES:

- ○ Calories 10
- ○ Protein <0.5g
- ○ Carbohydrate 2g
  Fibre <0.5g
- ○ Total Fat <0.5g
  Saturated Fat <0.5g
  Polyunsaturated Fat <0.5g
  Monounsaturated Fat <0.5g
- ○ Cholesterol 0mg
- ○ Sodium 28mg

Preparation Time: 10 minutes
Makes: 250ml (7fl oz)

MANGO SAUCE

DELICIOUS, VERSATILE, AND VIRTUALLY FAT-FREE, THIS FRUITY

SAUCE GIVES A VIBRANT COLOUR AND A CHILLI-HOT

FLAVOUR TO SALADS, MEAT, OR FISH.

1 small, ripe mango, peeled, stoned, and chopped
juice of 2 limes or 1 lemon
1 tbsp Dijon or English mustard
1 tsp finely grated lime or lemon zest
1 small chilli, deseeded and finely chopped (optional)
2 tbsp snipped fresh chives
salt and freshly ground black pepper, to taste

Place the mango flesh and lime juice in a food processor, and blend until smooth. (If the mango is too "stringy" press it through a fine sieve.) Add the remaining ingredients and seasoning, then mix well.

✳ STAR INGREDIENT
Although low in fat, skimmed milk retains useful amounts of protein, calcium, potassium, zinc, magnesium, folate, and vitamin C.

1 TABLESPOON PROVIDES:

○ Calories 22

○ Protein 1g

○ Carbohydrate 3g
  Fibre 0g

○ Total Fat <1g
  Saturated Fat <0.5g
  Polyunsaturated Fat <0.5g
  Monounsaturated Fat <0.5g

○ Cholesterol 21mg

○ Sodium 11mg

PREPARATION TIP
This salad cream will keep for up to a week if stored, covered, in the refrigerator.

Preparation Time: 15 minutes
Makes: 350ml (12fl oz)

ALMOST FAT-FREE SALAD CREAM

THIS SMOOTH, SILKY, AND SLIGHTLY PIQUANT SALAD CREAM IS
FULL OF FLAVOUR BUT IT HAS A FRACTION OF THE FAT OF MANY
SHOP-BOUGHT COUNTERPARTS.

2 egg yolks
1 tbsp English mustard powder
2 tbsp cornflour
1 tbsp caster sugar
½ tsp Tabasco
250ml (8fl oz) skimmed milk
100ml (3½fl oz) cider vinegar or white wine vinegar
salt, to taste

1 Whisk together the egg yolks, mustard, cornflour, sugar, and Tabasco in a heatproof bowl. Gradually whisk in the milk.

2 Place the bowl over a saucepan of simmering water. Cook, stirring frequently, for 5–8 minutes, until the sauce starts to thicken. Add the vinegar and seasoning, then continue to cook for 3–4 minutes, until smooth and creamy.

VARIATIONS

Fresh Herb Salad Cream Stir in 3–4 tablespoons chopped fresh mixed herbs, at the end of the cooking time in step 2, above.

Piquant Tomato Salad Cream Add 2 tablespoons of tomato purée, a clove of garlic, crushed, and ½ teaspoon chilli powder with the vinegar in step 2, above.

INDEX

Page numbers in **bold italics** indicate illustrations. Page numbers followed by an asterisk (*) indicate star ingredients.

NUTRITIONAL DATA

● The nutritional analyses accompanying the recipes are only approximate. They are based on data from food composition tables with additional information about manufactured products, not on direct analysis of the made-up dishes.

● Sometimes the figures for saturated and unsaturated fats do not equal the total fat figure. This is because the fat total includes other fatty acids and non-fatty acid compounds.

● The symbol "<1g" in the recipe nutritional analyses for the recipes indicates that there is less than 1 gram of the particular nutrient.

● All recipes have been analyzed on the basis of no added salt, unless specified in the recipe.

● Ingredients that are described as "optional" are not included in the nutritional analyses.

ACKNOWLEDGMENTS

Author's acknowledgments: I would like to dedicate this book to Saul, my best taster and washer-upper (and a heart patient). My gratitude also goes to the team: Nicola Graimes, Sue Storey, Jane Suthering, Ian O'Leary, Emma Brogli, and Alison Austin who made this book so delightful and fun to write.

Dorling Kindersley would like to thank Jasmine Challis for the nutritional analyses in the recipe section, Sue Bosanko for the index, and Janice Anderson, Stephanie Farrow, and Jude Garlick for editorial assistance.

Picture credits: the Body Mass Index Chart on page 12 and the Food Label on page 18 are based on material provided by the Diabetes UK picture library; food photography on pages.12–13 is by Andrew Whittuck.